"Cindy Reid not only has been great for the TPC at Sawgrass and the PGA Tour, she has done wonders for many individuals. I like to think I'm in good shape, but this book has shown me that I have a long way to go if I want to take my golf game to the next level."
—Tim Finchem, PGA Tour commissioner

"I've known Cindy for more than a decade. She's one of the best golf instructors I've ever seen and a model for the female golfer/athlete."
—Donna Orender, president of the WNBA

"I wish Cindy's book had been around when I first took up the game. Like a lot of guys my age, I never equated golf with physical fitness. I figured as long as you could bend over to put a tee in the ground, you were fit enough to play. Boy, was I wrong. This book is a real eye-opener. To play well, you must dedicate yourself to the game, practice, and work out. There is no gain without pain. There are many good rounds out there. Cindy will tell you how rewarding they can be."
—Jim Schiro, CEO of Zurich Financial Services

"Cindy and I first met almost 20 years ago, at a driving range, and became great friends. She went on to become a very successful golf instructor, and I, an exercise physiologist and trainer. This book has now brought both worlds together. Merely playing golf will *not* get you in Golf Shape, but *Get Yourself in Golf Shape* will get you playing better golf! Thanks, Cindy."
—Carolyn G. LeVan, M.A., C.S.C.S., certified strength and conditioning specialist

GET YOURSELF IN
GOLF SHAPE

Year-Round Drills
to Build a Strong, Flexible Swing

CINDY REID
with STEVE EUBANKS

FOREWORD BY VIJAY SINGH

RODALE

© 2005 by Cindy Reid and Steve Eubanks

All rights reserved. No part of this publication may be reproduced or transmitted in any form or by any means, electronic or mechanical, including photocopying, recording, or any other information storage and retrieval system, without the written permission of the publisher.

Printed in the United States of America
Rodale Inc. makes every effort to use acid-free ∞, recycled paper ♲.

Book design by Christopher Rhoads

Interior photographs by Mitch Mandel/Rodale Images, except for those otherwise credited.

Illustrations by Molly Borman

Library of Congress Cataloging-in-Publication Data

Reid, Cindy.
    Get yourself in golf shape : year-round drills to build a strong, flexible swing / Cindy Reid with Steve Eubanks; foreword by Vijay Singh.
        p.   cm.
    Includes index.
    ISBN-13 978–1–59486–188–8 paperback
    ISBN-10 1–59486–188–9 paperback
    1. Swing (Golf)   2. Golf.   I. Eubanks, Steve, date.   II. Title.
GV979.S9R43   2005
796.352'3—dc22   2005013082

Distributed to the trade by Holtzbrinck Publishers

4 6 8 10 9 7 5   paperback

We inspire and enable people to improve their lives and the world around them
For more of our products visit **rodalestore.com** or call 800-848-4735

To Mo Gregory

Only one person has touched us all at the TPC. Not the designer,

the commissioners, nor any of the superstar winners on the Tour.

The truest champion dedicated herself to making each of the days

we spent with her a little brighter, a little funnier.

You are loved, missed, and forever remembered.

Thank you, Mo.

CONTENTS

ACKNOWLEDGMENTS

Just as learning to play golf takes a lot of time, effort, and support from skilled teachers, writing a book about fitness and golf is every bit the team effort. The time spent in doing research, organizing thoughts, and putting them to paper consumed more of my days, weeks, and months than I could have imagined. Without my team, this project would have been unthinkable.

A very special thank-you goes out to my friend Jim. He has brought clarity to my goals, enthusiasm and encouragement to my projects, and the strength and confidence to complete them. Thank you for the countless hours.

To my friend and agent, Mark Reiter: When will you load up your right side and create enough power to hit it past me?

To my coauthor, Steve Eubanks, with whom I have collaborated on both of my books, thank you for your dedication and friendship. Now, go take some lessons and quit spending money on new drivers.

FOREWORD

I have only recently become one of golf's biggest proponents for fitness, realizing that playing at the highest levels requires top Tour players to be *athletes*. Early in my career I was a teaching professional. Then I became an accomplished winner on the professional Tour. However, there was a missing element that prevented me from realizing my ultimate potential. My fitness level was already somewhat above average on Tour, but I knew I needed more.

I hired a trainer, built a gym in my home, and set some achievable goals for conditioning, strength, and flexibility. To coin a phrase, I was getting "Golf Strong." The results were obvious and measurable. I won nine times in 2004, won the money title 2 years in a row, was awarded the Varden Trophy for the lowest stroke average, and became the number-one-ranked player in the world. Of course, not all of my good fortune came strictly from fitness. But I can assure you that, as I approached 40, without my improved conditioning, becoming the world's number one would still be a goal, not an accomplishment. In fact, the player I replaced at the top is also extremely physically fit. You may have heard of him.

Now, virtually every top-25 player is pursuing a higher level of fitness with great zeal and dedication. For the long haul in this increasingly demanding profession, there is no substitute for conditioning, strength, and flexibility. There are plenty of fundamentals you'll need to learn before you can become a successful golfer. Key among them is getting your body in shape to achieve and repeat a sound swing.

My friend Cindy Reid has understood and promoted the value of conditioning as well as any teacher in the game today. The drills outlined in these pages are a perfect complement to the hours you'll need to spend at the range to measurably improve your golf game and give you that "edge" you'll need stepping up to the first tee. If you want to play great golf, you'll need to be in great shape and work hard to stay there. This book is a great start to both of these goals.

—Vijay Singh
Ponte Vedra Beach, Florida

INTRODUCTION

My
name is Cindy Reid. I
teach people to play golf. I have
done so for 15 years, as the director of
instruction at the Tournament Players Club at
Sawgrass in Ponte Vedra Beach, Florida. I have
had the privilege of working with players of every
possible skill level, from absolute beginners to the
world's number-one-ranked PGA Tour player. Every
single student is unique, and every one has an interesting perspective on the game. Just as players' skill
levels vary, so too do their fitness levels. Is there
a connection between a golfer's quality of
play and his or her degree of fitness?
Historically, it would not appear so. But

today, ask yourself, "Are golfers athletes?" Let's explore that.

One of my students is a biomechanical engineer. He's a robot guy. His job is the study of the intricacies of human movement. This science helps create machines that replicate these motions for robotic workers in factories. During one of our recent lessons, he said something that piqued my interest.

"I've studied the swings of many great players, going back nearly 100 years," he said. "Harry Vardon, Bobby Jones, Hogan, Snead, Palmer, Nicklaus, Player, Watson, Norman, Faldo, Tiger—if there are pictures or film, I've analyzed them."

I hear this a lot, perhaps too often. A number of the people who come to me for instruction have spent time studying Tour players' swings in the hopes of finding golf's "secret" or, worse, a quick fix. Some even have swing sequence photographs framed and hanging in their dens. But this student's observations intrigued me. As a scientist who studies human movement for a living, he can write complex equations to explain how we pick up coffee cups and read the morning paper at the same time. If any student could provide unique insight into the golf swing, it should be him.

"What did you learn?" I asked.

"I was surprised," he said. "From a biomechanical perspective, the golf swing is a fairly simple motion. There's nothing superhuman about it. Jack Nicklaus could have lost a few pounds in his prime. Arnold Palmer and Nick Faldo looked like they could have played linebacker in the NFL. That aside, I found the physiques of great players to be very ordinary. And their swings were not extraordinary. Then, as now, the great swings are straightforward. This keeps me wondering, 'Why the hell can't I copy them?'"

This is the question that has plagued us for decades and the one that prompted me to write this book.

Golf is unique in that, just as my engineering student observed, the motions of the golf swing are fundamentally simple. There are no pirouettes or gravity-defying vertical leaps in our game. You don't have to have power-lifter biceps or Marion Jones's 100-meter speed to swing a golf club. Charles Howell III is one of the longest hitters in golf. He consistently booms drives in excess of 320 yards, fully 50 yards longer than the average golfer's best shot. So why is Howell, at 5 feet 10 inches and 155 pounds, able to hit the ball so much farther than you or I? And what about power players like Adam Scott, Phil Mickelson, and Davis Love III? What's their secret? On the surface, these players don't appear to be bigger or stronger than the average amateur golfer. When Love was a senior at the University of North Carolina, he was certainly not a finely tuned physical specimen, yet he could move the ball a long, long way. Today's great players are not built like NFL quarterback Michael Vick or baseball great

Mark McGwire. There was even a time when my friend (the now *very* fit) Vijay Singh could have skipped a few meals.

Then there are the women. How can Karrie Webb and Annika Sorenstam consistently drive the ball farther than even the most accomplished male amateur? And more important, what prevents amateurs from *ever* achieving the power that Love, Couples, Webb, and Sorenstam make look so effortless?

The answer is as simple as the problem itself.

The greats of our game are not physically imposing, and until recently, few of them even looked fit. But they have trained their bodies to find the *fundamental positions* of a good golf swing and to do so with maximum speed and efficiency. Anyone who has ever watched the practice tee at a PGA Tour event recognizes the beauty of the professional golf swing. The motions are like flawlessly choreographed ballet: an art form, fluid and effortless. Great golf swings are, as Sam Snead used to describe them, "oily." They look as natural as flowing water, yet they produce prodigious, even explosive power. How can this be the same game so many amateurs struggle to play with even a modicum of consistency?

One's ability to bench-press 300 pounds or inability to lift a golf bag out of the trunk has little or no bearing on learning the *fundamentals* of a sound swing. The reason Charles, Davis, Phil, Karrie, Adam Scott, and teenage sensation Michelle Wie hit the ball consis-

tently farther than we do is simple: We have not physically trained our bodies to find golf's fundamental positions. They have.

Like my biomechanical-engineering student, I too have studied most of the game's greats, and have come to the realization that the greatest players in history share a high degree of consistency at seven key positions. These positions can be found in the tweed-coat, wool-tie, and hickory-shaft swings of Harry Vardon and Bobby Jones, through the persimmon-heads and unforgiving-irons era of Ben Hogan and Sam Snead. The power game of Arnold Palmer and Jack Nicklaus and today's modern athletic golf swings of Tiger Woods and Ernie Els still rely on hitting these spots every time.

On the surface, many of these players' swings look somewhat different. Side-by-side, significant differences exist between Hogan's flat, slashing swing and the long, fluid motion of Ernie Els. Palmer and Davis Love look like they read entirely different how-to books on golf. But at *seven points* during their swings, they are all brothers in perfection, just like the robots of my biomechanical engineer. Those seven fundamental positions are:

1. Address
2. Initial takeaway
3. Top of the backswing
4. Initial downswing
5. Impact

Scott Halleran/Getty Images

The American Golfer

Tiger Woods at the top of his backswing   Ben Hogan at the top of his backswing

6. Extension

7. Finish (Okay, maybe not Arnie's!)

Am I saying that Ben Hogan's and Tiger Woods's swings look the same at the top of their backswings? Well, not entirely. Hogan was a shade over 5 feet 8 and weighed 145 pounds (thus the nickname Bantam Ben), while Woods is 6 feet 2 and a fit 190 pounds. Hogan played with heavy persimmon woods and sharp, upright irons, with shafts that you would give away at a garage sale. Woods plays with the most high-tech equipment today's design engineers can create. Woods has received instruction and tutelage from the greatest teachers in the game since he was a child. Hogan had to, in his words, "dig (the golf swing) out of the dirt."

Sure, their swings are bound to look different, yet at the top, both men have made full shoulder turns around relatively quiet hips. Both have turned their heads slightly to facilitate that full shoulder rotation, yet maintained a "level" head position. They have kept their heads well behind the ball at the top, and both have loaded most of their weight onto their right sides. Their knees are flexed and their legs taut, providing a solid base from which to begin the downswing. And, like most great ball strikers, their left arms are relatively straight, but not rigid. The spine angle of both players has remained constant and relatively straight throughout the backswing. At the top, both players have the shaft pointing toward the target. Yes, their swings may appear to be different, but at the top they have more commonalities than differences.

The same is true for all great players at all seven of the fundamental positions in the swing. Arnold Palmer and Ernie Els couldn't be more different in terms of their style of play. Palmer attacked the golf ball with a hard hitting motion many compared to a lumberjack assaulting a redwood. Els's swing, with his relaxed rhythm, creates tremendous clubhead speed, which belies his "oily" tempo. However, photographs of both men at impact are remarkably similar, if not identical.

My engineering student recognized this. In fact, so do most of my moti-

vated, if not scientifically inclined, students. You don't have to be a great player to know what a great swing looks like.

The problem, I have found, isn't the lack of knowledge; it's the fact that most amateurs have not trained their bodies to swing the club to the same seven key positions they see with the game's top players. They sit hunched over their desks all day, yet expect not to slouch when they set up to hit a golf shot. They use the small muscles of their hands and arms to lift their phones, coffee cups, staplers, and file folders, yet they hope those same muscles won't take over their golf swing. They know their big muscles should dominate and hope that somehow, as if through sheer will, these same muscles will put the club in the right places.

Well, without some training, that won't happen. Even those who hit the gym regularly work out in a way that tightens, shortens, and strengthens muscles—counterproductive to a good golf swing. As a result, their strength works against them. Their speed is applied in the wrong places, and the stronger muscles overpower the *correct* muscles needed in a fluid swing. Show me cut abs, pumped chests, and huge biceps, and I'll show you restricted swings, bad shots, and big scores. Such players exert a lot of effort with limited results.

This is not to imply that motivated amateurs are physically incapable of making good golf swings. Many will scoff at my earlier proclamation that the golf swing is simple, but it's true. Biomechanically speaking, the golf swing is a simple motion. Anybody and everybody can make a good golf swing if they are willing to train their bodies. However, a fundamentally sound swing, though simple, is not easy. While "simple" means uncomplicated and straightforward, "easy" implies that a good swing does not require work and dedication.

A good swing is not a "natural" athletic move, like throwing a ball or stroking a tennis forehand. In fact, a golf swing is one of the most unnatural motions in sports. Starting from a rest, you coil your upper body around your spine and right leg, while transferring your weight to one side. Simultaneously, you raise the club over your head to a position that you cannot see. Then, you merely uncoil your shoulders, torso, and hips in the opposite direction, around that still-stationary spine, and transfer all your weight to the other side. In the meantime, you've accelerated a blob of titanium on the end of a 4-foot metal shaft to a hundred miles per hour. Oh yeah, did I mention that the clubhead must come back perfectly square, to *exactly* where it started from? That you must maintain Baryshnikov-like balance while hitting a dime-size sweet spot on a 1.68-inch ball? All this happens in about 2 seconds. And to top it all off, you must convince yourself to stay relaxed during this anything-but-relaxed gyration.

Does anything about that sound "easy"? Of course not. Everything about the golf swing fights your natural instincts. You hit down on the ball in order for it to go up. You swing the club right of the target in order for the ball to curve left. You must remove tension from your hands and arms in order to strike the ball harder and hit it farther. Pros stand tall while hitting a stationary object sitting on the ground, and they rotate their shoulders around a reasonably straight spine. Have you thought about your spine angle lately? It's not something that pops into your head as you're brushing your teeth in the morning. Spine angle is even overlooked while you watch a video of your own swing. ("Yikes, whose crummy swing did they digitally attach to my head?") But accomplished golfers have trained their bodies to create these unnatural motions. *Great* players can repeat these motions, consistently putting the club into the seven key positions.

The golf swing is simple, but golf is the hardest game in the world at which to excel—much less, dare I say, master. Sometimes, the game just seems to come to you, and good scores come easy. As quickly as they came, however, facets begin to slip away, and that magical "zone" is lost. As anyone who has ever played the game will attest, just when you think you've got it all together, a mistake here, an errant shot there, humble you mercilessly. The motion that seemed so natural and fluid yesterday gets disjointed and unsynchronized. Gone is the confidence that made the fairways look as wide as Montana and the cups as big as manholes. You begin to second-guess your mechanics. Rhythm and timing seem lost, and the cup shrinks to a pinhole. Everybody who has ever played the game has been there, and everyone, even the Tour pros, will be there again. This is what will forever keep us from that mythical spot called perfect. Imagine, will anyone ever birdie all 18 holes in a PGA event? This is why we practice, buy new clubs, talk endlessly about the game, then practice a little more. It's the great nature of the game.

Don't be fooled. You can't "conceptualize" your way to lower scores. Reading this book won't magically turn you into a Tour player. Simply reading it may not lower your handicap over night. There are plenty of "snake-oil" fixes and infomercials out there. This book is neither. I will walk you through the seven fundamental positions of golf, explaining the importance of each. Hopefully, I will help unravel the biomechanical mysteries of the golf swing by showing you how to train your body to find seven positions reflexively. Through simple exercises, stretches, and driving-range drills, I

will show you how to condition yourself to become a better, more consistent golfer. We will make your time on the practice tee more productive and more enjoyable.

Most of the exercises and stretches in this book can (and should) be performed away from the golf course and virtually every day of the week. For example, you can improve your address position while sitting at your desk. You can work on your finish while standing at the water cooler or waiting in line at the department of motor vehicles. None of these drills requires you to look like an idiot, and you won't be embarrassed in public. (Okay, you might draw some stares if you actually do them at the DMV.) But you *will* train your body to make a better golf swing.

Training your body to find the seven fundamental positions of the swing is the key to a great game of golf. Golf is work, and good golf is a lot of work. But working smarter, not harder, will make your valuable time on your practice facility more productive. The point of all this is to meet—and raise—your expectations and lower your scores, but most important, to enjoy the game like you never have before.

Let's get started.

GOLF SHAPE

A
couple of months after
he underwent arthroscopic knee
surgery, reporters asked Tiger Woods
about his health. His answer was telling. "The
knee feels good," he said. "I've been working out
and haven't had any trouble with it, but I don't
know if I'm in Golf Shape yet. There's a big differ-
ence between working out in the gym and being in
Golf Shape. I'm getting there. I'm really close. I've
just got to work myself back into a routine."
What on earth was Tiger talking about? What
is Golf Shape, and how does it differ from
any other kind of shape?
To answer that, you have to
rethink your

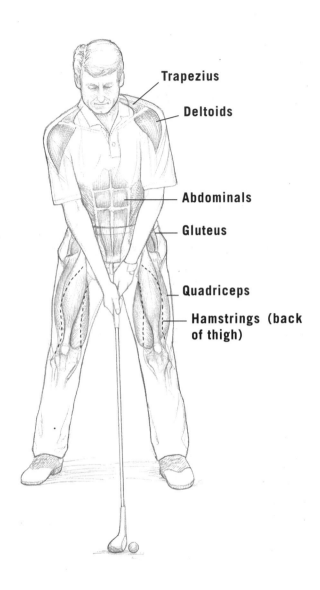

Trapezius

Deltoids

Abdominals

Gluteus

Quadriceps

Hamstrings (back of thigh)

concept of conditioning. Too many of us think that being in good condition is like being pregnant: Either you are or you aren't. This assumption is not true. As a golf instructor, I've had the opportunity to teach some fairly prominent athletes, including NFL Hall of Fame running back Marcus Allen and NBA great Charles Barkley. Those guys will tell you what I've known for years: Being in Golf Shape is not the same thing as being in what we have traditionally thought of as good physical shape. A marathon runner isn't, by default, in Golf Shape. Conversely, most golfers can't finish a marathon. Marcus and Charles are great athletes who have kept themselves in good physical condi-

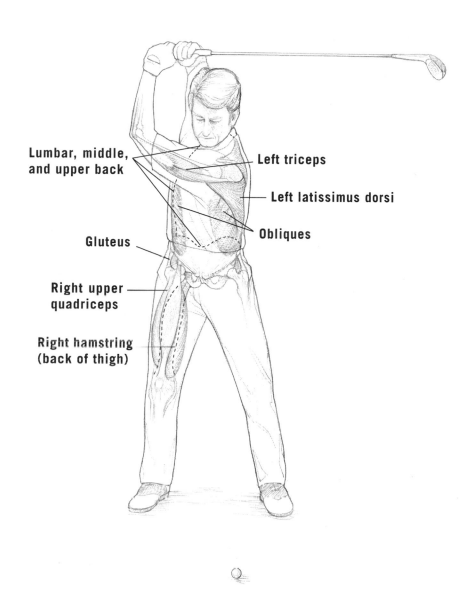

Lumbar, middle, and upper back

Left triceps

Left latissimus dorsi

Gluteus

Obliques

Right upper quadriceps

Right hamstring (back of thigh)

tion (even though Charles has put on a few pounds), but after a day or two on the driving range, they will be the first to admit they aren't in great Golf Shape.

The golf swing requires you to use muscles that you might not use in any other activity (see the illustrations on pages 10 through 13): muscles like the pronator quadratus, a small muscle in the forearm that allows you to pronate and supinate your arm. Unless you spend all day rotating your hands palms up to palms down, you probably haven't trained your pronator quadratus to make a consistent golf swing. The same is true with the rectus abdominis, the abdominal muscle between

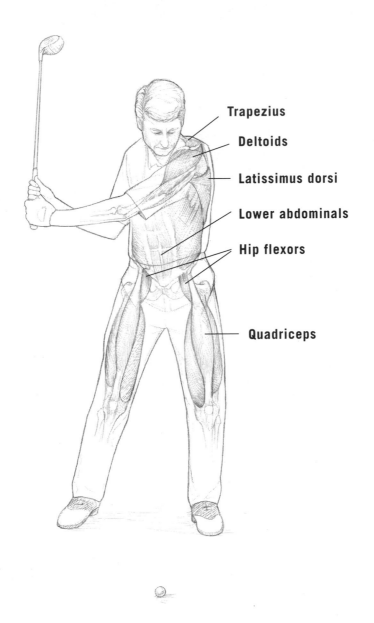

Trapezius

Deltoids

Latissimus dorsi

Lower abdominals

Hip flexors

Quadriceps

your navel and your groin. Unless you're in the North Korean army and marching in the goosestep every day, you probably haven't trained your rectus abdominis in a way that's conducive to a good, consistent golf swing. Rotator cuffs, lateral obliques, latis-simus dorsi—these are all muscles you use in unique ways when swinging a golf club. Unless your swing is sound and you are hitting practice balls every day, those muscles probably aren't in Golf Shape.

Getting yourself in Golf Shape means

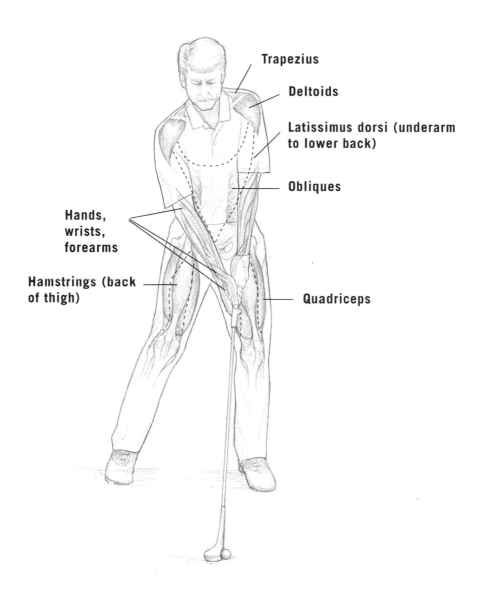

Trapezius

Deltoids

Latissimus dorsi (underarm to lower back)

Obliques

Hands, wrists, forearms

Hamstrings (back of thigh)

Quadriceps

training your muscles to move a certain way without having to think about it. You've also heard it referred to as muscle memory, a phrase widely accepted by most professional coaches and instructors. Granted, true memory resides only in the human brain.

Muscle memory simply refers to training your muscles to perform a task, and repeat that task, until it becomes second nature. You don't have to think about the mechanics of opening a jar of peanut butter. Your hands and wrist "just do it." You don't have to concentrate on how hard to press the gas pedal to accelerate to (or in Sergio Garcia's case, well beyond) the speed limit. You've stepped on the gas often enough that the motion is automatic. The same can be true of your golf swing, provided you have trained golf-specific muscles. If your swing muscles put the club in the same positions (rightly or wrongly) over years of practice, your basic golf moves are now in muscle memory.

Once your muscles commit a movement to memory, they will resist change. If you don't believe this, try going up a set of stairs by stepping first with the opposite foot from the one you normally start with. Feels unnatural, doesn't it? This is classic muscle memory.

How lucky we would all be if all the golf moves we engrained early on were fundamentally correct (like Tiger's). Our muscle memories would know a great swing, and this book wouldn't be necessary. Fortunately for you, in the following chapters I provide a physical training program that will retrain your body so that the seven fundamental positions become second nature. Follow this program, and I guarantee you'll finally be able to say you're in Golf Shape.

Let's Get Real

Any time I'm teaching a student for the first time, my first question is: "What do you hope to accomplish?"

More often than not, the answer is, "I want to be consistent."

I've heard this so many times I've become glib in my response. "Okay," I say. "You need to hit 1,000 balls a day for the next 5 months. You should hit 50 balls with every club in your bag in the morning, break for lunch, then do the same thing in the afternoon."

This is usually met by an open-mouthed look of disbelief and an occasional "Come on!" or unprintable comeback.

"I'm serious," I say. "I didn't just pull that regimen out of my hat. Ben Hogan, thought by most to be the most consistent ball striker of his or any era, did that for most of his professional career. On the days Hogan didn't hit 1,000 balls, he hit 500 balls in the morning and played in the afternoon. That's what it takes to achieve consistency in this game."

Once the shock wears off, I say, "Now, let's get real."

Call it what you like—shock therapy, over-the-top total golf immersion, or just plain hard core—but I call it realism. Most new golfers give up a serious pursuit of the game within a year of taking their first lesson, because they set unrealistic expectations and get frustrated when they don't meet those pie-in-the-sky goals. I can't tell you the number of times a student has said something like, "I want to break 80," or "I want to be competitive in my club championship." But when he or she comes back for the second, third, and fourth lessons, without practicing between those lessons, real progress is limited and the original swing errors have crept back in.

"How often have you practiced since your last lesson?" I ask.

"Well, I played twice," is a typical response.

So I spend an hour repeating myself and going through the same drills my student and I worked on before.

New golfers are notorious for setting unreasonable expectations. An 8-handicapper who hasn't practiced in 2 months wonders why he can't break 80 in his first rounds of the season; an 18-handicapper who goes straight from the lesson tee to the first tee can't figure out why she hasn't shaved 5 strokes off her score; and a player who shanks his sand shots wonders why that short-game article he read on the train last week didn't cure him of this dreaded malady.

Golfers experience that same gap between expectations and reality in their fitness regimens, if they even have them. A golfer who doesn't stretch or strengthen golf-specific muscles and warm up properly wonders why he's played three or four holes before he's established any rhythm. Fatigue replaces focus, and the last several holes come unglued. As we say in this scenario, "The wheels have come off his trolley." Conditioning has never occurred to him. All the post-round swing analysis in the world will not solve the problem. He's not out of breath, and he doesn't feel exhausted, so how could his problems be fitness-related?

Sure, you may not "feel" tired, but the muscles used to swing the golf club fatigue, and your body's ability to put the club in the correct positions begins to diminish. You might rally for a hole or two, drawing on your favorite temporary, quick fix, but as the round progresses, you're approaching the point of breakdown. Okay, you're not panting, sweating profusely, or holding your sides, but your golf muscles are shot. The muscle memory that had put the club where it needed to be is lost, the rhythm is gone, and your good round is essentially over.

So, let's get real. Before you can focus on the seven positions, you need to commit to your conditioning. Here are seven rules for getting in, and staying in, Golf Shape.

Cindy's Seven Rules for Getting in Golf Shape

Rule #1: Spend an equal or greater number of hours on golf-specific fitness and conditioning as you do on your golf swing.

If you hit balls for 1 hour twice a week, spend at least that amount of time on improving your golf fitness. This doesn't mean you can skip a workout if you miss a practice session. It means you should split your time equally between practicing golf and keeping your body in Golf Shape. Rather than hitting balls for 2 hours, hit balls for 1 hour and spend the remaining hour working on the exercises in this book.

I don't expect you to become a super-athlete. If you're not a decathlete now, you won't become one after implementing the fitness program outlined in these pages (though it would be a great start). You will, however, be physically equipped to shoot lower scores.

Rule #2: Never hit the first ball without stretching.

If I have to choose between hitting practice balls for half an hour or stretching, I'll take stretching every time. After all, the sound mechanics of your swing are in muscle memory, right? I like to schedule 15 extra minutes prior to my warmup session to go through many of the stretches outlined in this book. If I'm pressed for time, I'll stretch for 15 minutes and hit balls for 10. If I am *really* pressed for time, I'll spend that time stretching and go to the tee without hitting a single practice shot. I may stretch out those first-shot muscles by slowly and smoothly swinging my driver with a hand towel wrapped around the clubhead (even just attaching my golf glove around the hosel will add some resistance—much more on this idea later).

However, unless I have *completely* overslept, I will always find a few minutes to roll a few putts.

You will always play better after stretching. Think back to the last time you rushed through a small bucket just before your tee time. Most of those shots were awful anyway, right? You didn't really accomplish much. In fact, don't we all use the expression "I'm going to the practice tee to warm up"? So stretch a while to *warm up,* and release that fluid swing you've worked so hard to develop.

In a perfect world, I would arrive at the practice facility 45 minutes before my tee time. I would stretch for 15 minutes, then begin my practice-shot regimen until I know I'm on deck. The last minute would be set aside to hit the shot I intend to hit on the first tee. But we'll get into these finer points in a later book.

Rule #3: Begin your practice sessions close to the hole and work your way out.

A golfer's natural urge is to pick up the driver as quickly as possible. You hustle out to the practice tee to warm up before your round, and the first (or maybe second or third) swing is with the longest club in your bag. Does this make sense? Would you start out your tennis warmup with a booming overhead smash? How about starting out a 3-mile jog with a flat-out 200-yard sprint? Just doesn't sound right, does it? Not only is it counterproductive, you stand a very good chance of hurting yourself.

The most effective practice and warmup sessions start with short putts of no more than 3 feet. From there, move back to 5 or 6 feet, then 10 feet, and then hit a few 30-footers before adjourning to the practice tee where you should start with pitch shots of no more than 50 yards. After a handful of short pitches at no particular target, you can extend your swing with a wedge to hit the ball 80 yards, 100 yards, then finally, to your maximum accurate range. This is a good time to introduce a specific target to your wedge practice. Once you've hit several full wedges, you can move up through your bag.

I always warm up with a lob wedge, a pitching wedge, a 7 iron, 5 iron, 3 iron, and finally, the driver. The same is true when I'm practicing after a round, or simply going through a stand-alone practice session. The longest club in the bag is the last one I hit, not the first. Even if I'm on the tee specifically to work on my driver, I always start the session with short irons and work up to the driver.

This is not a unique routine. However, there are a few notable golf teachers who alter this sequence somewhat. It is largely a matter of preference. Most Tour players, however, stick to this regimen in both their warmups and their lengthy practice sessions. Even players like Jason Zuback, four-time world long-drive champion and someone who makes his living hitting the ball long and hard, never hits driver without warming up with a wedge, an 8 iron, and a 5 iron.

As a member of the Hall of Fame, Nick Price puts it: "The driver is the truth serum. When your driver's going awry, something's wrong with your swing." It's always better to hone your swing on the short clubs before pulling the "truth serum" out of your bag. If something goes a little ugly with the wedge, it will be *really* ugly with a driver. But let's be positive. Those perfect little wedges now will be dead-solid drives later.

Rule #4: Ease into a practice routine.

I can't tell you the number of students who go months without picking up a club and then a week before the company golf outing head to the range with a milk crate full of practice balls. After the second hour, they become exhausted and their swings fall apart. But they don't stop. These driving-range gladiators are determined to get better before they tee it up with their officemates. So they hit balls until they are cross-eyed and can barely lift their arms. The next day they have trouble crawling out of bed. Swinging a golf club on day two is out of the question.

If you haven't ridden a bicycle in 6 months, you don't go out for a 100-mile ride. Why treat golf differently?

Shorter and more frequent practice sessions are always better than daylong golf marathons. If you have a week to get ready for your big round, practice

30 minutes a day instead of 3 hours in a single afternoon. You'll see improvement in your stamina, and ultimately, a better scorecard.

Rule #5: Golf shouldn't hurt; stop playing if it does.

Golf is not a contact sport. You don't see any "no pain, no gain" posters on locker room walls at golf clubs, and you rarely see anyone carted off the golf course because of a game-related injury.

But that doesn't mean you can't injure yourself playing golf. Like any repetitive motion, the golf swing takes a toll on certain muscles and joints. Elbows, hands (primarily thumbs), and lower backs are most susceptible to injury. They are the body parts most strained by the motions of the golf swing and the ones least accustomed to this kind of exertion.

When you hurt your back or feel a pang in your elbow, wrist, or hand, the worst thing you can do is try to "play through it." Professionals, on occasion, *have* to play with minor injuries, to pay the bills. I cannot think of a single reason for an amateur to do the same. Most golf injuries stem from strained tendons or ligaments, so playing through the injury will only inflame them. When golf begins to hurt, call it a day.

Rule #6: Save the adult beverages for after the round.

The game is hard enough with all your faculties intact. A drink or two in the middle of the round adds shots to your score. Period. You may think it will relax you, but you will lose focus, coordination, and all your side bets. Plus, alcohol dehydrates your already taxed body, robbing you of vital liquids and nutrients. My advice to all students is to save the frosty brew for the 19th hole. A cold one always goes down better after you've posted a good score.

Rule #7: *Every day* do something to improve your golf game.

Unless you are retired, living on a golf course, or paid to play golf, you probably don't practice or play every day. But that shouldn't stop you from working on your game. Whether it's performing the exercises outlined in these pages, rolling some 10-foot putts on your bedroom carpet, working on your setup in front of the bathroom mirror, or swinging a club in your basement, you can work on *some* part of your game every day, all year long.

Think of Yourself as an Athlete, Not Just a Golfer

One day in the mid-1950s, Tommy Bolt, the fiery former U.S. Open champion, was standing on the first tee at a PGA Tour event with a cigarette dangling from his lips. A spectator said to Bolt, "I didn't think athletes smoked."

Bolt pointed a crooked finger at the onlooker and said, "I'm not an athlete; I'm a golfer."

While funny, that story held a kernel of truth through most of the previous century. Golfers weren't considered athletes, and golf wasn't considered an athletic endeavor. It was a game, not a sport—more akin to horseshoes or billiards than to more serious pursuits like football, basketball, baseball, soccer, or track and field.

Today we know better. The most successful professional players in the 21st century are keenly aware of the role of fitness in their continued success. Modern players have the same fitness goals—strength, speed, flexibility, balance, and endurance—as any other professional (especially winning) athletes. They have added strength training and cardiovasular exercise to their daily practice routines. This has paved the way for the PGA to include well-outfitted fitness trailers at every professional event. Because of these changes, today's golfers hit the ball farther than their predecessors and shoot lower scores than ever before.

It's no accident that Tiger Woods now holds the scoring records in all four of golf's major championships. Tiger is arguably more talented than anyone else who has ever played the game, but he is also extremely fit.

His regular routine includes weight training, endurance workouts, and flexibility drills. He works on every muscle group and spends more time on a treadmill and stationary bike than most people spend on the driving range. During the middle of his record-setting major-championship run in 2000, Tiger, once again, played well enough in the first three rounds to be in the final group at the PGA Championship. So how did he spend his Saturday night? After hitting balls until it was so dark he needed the lights from a CNN camera crew to see where his shots were landing, Tiger went straight to the gym where he spent the better part of 2 hours working with his trainer. Only after he had completed his workout did he go to his rented house for dinner and a couple of video games before bed. The next day, he became the first man since Ben Hogan in 1953 to win three of golf's majors in a single year.

Stories such as these are common now. Vijay Singh, having been a good player with a fine record, added a state-of-the-art gym onto his house. Since then, when not out on Tour, he has worked out 2 hours a day, three times a week. In 2004, he became the number-one player in the world, in the Sony rankings. And who did he edge out to become number one, you ask? Go back and read the previous paragraph again.

Davis Love III never lifted weights in his life until he hit his thirties. Now he works out consistently and has experienced the greatest success of his career.

Annika Sorenstam was a great player before she started working out, but it wasn't until she embarked on a full-fledged strength-and-fitness program that she became a record-setter. In 2 short years, Annika dramatically increased her strength and improved her flexibility and endurance. She accomplished these goals through selective weight training, stretching exercises, and rigorous cardiovascular workouts. To keep up, Se Ri Pak, Laura Diaz, and many other players have hired personal trainers and embarked on exercise regimens of their own. According to Pak, "Everybody is doing it now. If we want to stay where we are, we have to work that much more."

Ernie Els was another golfer who didn't believe he needed to be in shape to play. "I was determined to play golf professionally and not worry about being in great shape," Els said. "I was young enough and stupid enough to think that I'd never get out of shape and, anyway, golf wasn't all that physically demanding. I was lazy. Golf was fun. I loved spending hours on the golf course, but that was play, not work."

Then Ernie's natural abilities fell prey to his lack of fitness. In 1995 he carried a 3-shot lead into the final round of the PGA Championship and finished a distant third. In the British Open, he shot 75 in the final round and lost by 4 shots. He was getting tired at the wrong times (is there a "right" time?), losing focus and hitting too many loose shots.

"I realized I needed conditioning," Els said. "The game was getting more competitive, and the good golfers, the ones who were winning, were in shape. And there was Gary Player, my idol, at 62 still looking great, playing and winning. He is in shape. I decided it was time to finally step up and quit kidding myself. I had to get into shape. The game itself had changed. It was more athletic than it had ever been. I had to raise my body to the challenge."

Els did just that, working out regularly with a trainer and making a complete lifestyle change to accommodate his physical needs. Did it work? According to Els, "My swing now has more speed. My shot making is a lot more consistent. I have more power and flexibility, and I feel looser and stronger." He also won the 2002 British Open, picked up five worldwide victories, and won over $8 million in a single season. Being in better shape paid huge dividends to Ernie.

There are no excuses for not getting in and staying in Golf Shape. Neither Jack nor Arnie worked out with weights until joining the Senior Tour. "I never lifted a weight until I was 50," Palmer admitted. "I always stayed in shape through hard work, but I never worked out until I realized that, as I got older, I needed more strength and flexibility if I was going to continue to compete." Could any discussion about golf fitness be complete without mentioning Gary Player, the Dalai Lama of daily training to stay "golf fit"? (More on Gary later.) These fine players did it; so can you.

There isn't an excuse I haven't heard. The most common are: "I'm too old," "I'm too young," "I'm too weak," "I'm already strong enough," "I'm a woman," "I'm a kid," "Lifting weights will leave me too tight to play," and my all-time favorite: "I just don't have the time."

How about spending 20 minutes in the living room stretching, rather than standing in line at Starbuck's for a fat-free latte, thinking *that* will help you lose weight? It's not about having the time; it's about prioritizing.

Scrap the excuses. It's time to make a new commitment to improve your golf game, your general health, and your life. No matter what your age, gender, body type, strength level, or workout history, you can get in better Golf Shape and train your body to find the seven fundamental positions. Doing so will lower your scores. All it takes is commitment.

In the chapters that follow, I will step you through the seven fundamental po-sitions of a sound swing. We will explore specific exercises and drills to achieve Golf Shape, to enhance each position and your overall swing fitness. A relatively modest financial invest-ment in a gym membership or a few pieces of workout equipment that you may already have stashed in your garage (a physioball, light dumbbells, an elastic resistance band, a stretching bar, a medicine ball, a soccer ball, a tennis ball, an old driver, and stretching ropes) will pay off very quickly. We are all prepared to spend hundreds, if not thousands, of dollars on the newest golf equipment, trying to buy an improved game. Why not spend just a few dollars on exercise equip-ment to absolutely guarantee better scores? I'll also explain the importance of adding stretching to your daily schedule, regardless of how often you practice. And finally, I'll lay out an 11-day workout program to help you budget the time you must spend to get yourself in Golf Shape.

POSITION ONE
SETUP

Jack Nicklaus believes that a good setup is 80 percent of the battle in hitting a good golf shot. Far be it from me to disagree with Jack, but I would put that number at closer to 90 percent. Setup and grip, which are discussed in detail in my first book, *Cindy Reid's Ultimate Guide to Golf for Women*, are the most important essentials in golf, the cornerstones on which every shot is built. That's why Tour players spend so much time on their setups. Players like Phil Mickelson and Jim Furyk train their caddies to check their posture and positions at address. Vijay Singh and Stuart Appleby work with training aids and drills to maintain their setups. In fact, virtually all advanced players have someone with a trained eye check their setups on a regular basis. If you walk the driving range on any professional Tour, you'll even find players getting setup advice from fellow pros. Rarely is advice given about swing mechanics, but you will always hear setup, setup, setup.

The reason for this obsession with the setup is simple: As I tell all my students, you can make an average swing from a good setup and still hit a good shot. However, from a poor setup, the quality of your swing is irrelevant, and the chances of consistently hitting good shots are nil.

This indisputable fact of golf explains why so many well-meaning amateurs struggle. No matter how hard they work, how much self-analysis they do, or how many magazines they read, most amateurs can't "cure their slice," "hit it farther," or "get it up and down every time." It's not because they don't understand what to do, but because their bodies won't allow a proper setup, done repeatedly.

The Posture Paradox

A majority of amateurs try to play golf from awkward yet, to them, seemingly natural and comfortable positions. Unfortunately, most of these positions are technically flawed and make putting the club in any of our seven key positions a crapshoot, at best. You've probably stepped onto the first tee and immediately ticked through the mental checklist you've been taught. Firm left arm, shoulders back, head still, chin up, knees flexed, butt out . . . now relax and swing! Right? What can go wrong now?

The truth is, you are probably not in *any* of those positions.

One reason most golfers struggle with their games is that the proper golf setup runs contrary to the average player's natural posture. The golf ball is on the ground, so the inclination of all humans is to round the back and slump the shoulders in order to hit it. The ball is also sitting still, not coming toward you or moving away from you, so your instinct is to assume the same narrow stance you would use in the checkout line at the grocery store. Rarely in everyday life do you bow at the waist, keeping your back straight, your chin up, and your shoulders tall and square. I can think of very few everyday-life activities where you stand with your feet shoulder width apart, knees slightly flexed, with the majority of your weight on the balls of your feet, and your left hip slightly higher than your right. Those are the positions of a proper setup, positions you rarely practice or experience anywhere other than the golf course.

It's a sad fact, but most people have poor posture in their everyday lives. If you're sitting down right now, check your posture. Are your shoulder blades drawn back and down? Is your stomach drawn up and in? Are your ears on the same vertical plane as your hips? And how much space is between your chin and your chest? You get the idea.

Since you probably don't practice great posture in your everyday life, how can you expect your body to assume a healthy, athletic posture over a golf ball? Your muscles aren't conditioned properly, so you revert to what feels natural and comfortable: a stiff, hunched position, from which swinging a club to our seven fundamental positions is all but impossible.

How Difficult Can It Be?

Average golfers pay scant attention to their setups, because:

(a) They cannot mentally connect the dots between setup and a technically sound swing.

(b) They cannot see their setup position from most key angles.

Besides, it just doesn't sound that difficult. You aren't being asked to perform yoga, assume a ballet position, or defend themselves in a fencing duel. Of course, like many things in life, it is a matter of perspective and discipline. It can be as easy as you are willing to make it, or it can be made difficult by letting old habits or lack of effort dictate your results. Some of us are just plain stubborn.

It's true that from a physical standpoint, a good setup is not terribly demanding. You don't have to balance on your toes like a ballerina or hold an iron cross like a gymnast. I reiterate, stand with your feet shoulder width apart, knees slightly flexed, bend at the hips so that your back remains reasonably straight, keep your chin up, and grip the club so that your left shoulder is slightly higher than your right. Your head should be positioned behind the ball.

This sounds simple because it really is. In fact, the golf setup is not that different from the stance and posture used by a basketball player shooting a free throw or by a good skier carving a turn. Try to think of it as a "weight-on-the-balls-of-your-feet, ready-to-do-something-athletic" posture. To really understand the importance of this, try sitting back on your heels, then try a basketball jump shot. Did you get very high? Did you leave the ground at all? I doubt it. It's simply not possible. Only Phil Mickelson, on the 18th green after having just won the Masters, jumped worse than you just did.

What makes a proper setup feel so strange is that it *is* different from most of your daily stances. For example, if you're standing by the water cooler at work, by the coffeepot in your kitchen, or in line at the local cineplex, you're probably doing so in a way that feels comfortable and natural. Your hips might be cocked to one side. You might even have your hands in your pockets. Your feet are probably close together, and unless you're a soldier or a runway model, your back is likely to be curved and your shoulders slouched. Sound familiar? This is how most people stand, or sit, around the home or office.

It's also counterproductive to the athleticism required for a good golf swing.

As if the setup itself were not unnatural enough, adding a golf club to the mix creates a whole new host of problems. To prove it, clasp your hands together in front of your chest. If you want, simulate a golf grip, although it is not necessary for this demonstration.

When most of you put your hands together like this, you "close" your chest, and the tendency is to round your shoulders and spine even further,

assuming that hunched-over slouch. Now, let's begin the correction. Keeping your hands together, stick your chest out (the feeling of "opening" it), straighten your back, and think about squeezing your shoulder blades together. This may seem somewhat unnatural (since you've spent most of your waking hours slouched over), but you have just begun to improve your posture for setup. Look at a picture of a pro's setup, and you'll "feel" what he has learned to do over every shot. Now, you'll begin to believe. But, if while holding this book in front of you, your back is rounded and your shoulders are hunched forward, you've slipped back to the natural position we tend to assume every day.

Setting up with poor posture

It feels very natural, but it is certainly terrible for your golf game and your life in general.

Here's another valuable demonstration: Place an item—this book, a glass, or a paperweight—on the edge of a table, desk or counter. Now stand about 3 feet away from the item, far enough away that you can't reach it from an upright position, but close enough that you can lean forward and pick it up. Without moving your feet, lean forward and grab the item from the counter. Ninety-nine percent of people round their spines and lower their shoulders in making this motion. They usually lower their chins as well.

Now, place the item back on the table and pick it up again. Only this time keep your chin up, your tummy tucked, and your back perfectly straight.

If you're like most people, the first time you try this, it may not be immediately obvious that the only way to do this (and stay balanced) is to bow from the hips and flex your knees slightly. After a few tries, doing so will seem perfectly natural.

Here's another example: Stand and look at a spot or an object on the floor a few feet in front of you. Unless you are wearing a neck brace, you probably looked down by bending your neck and lowering your chin toward your chest. You have lowered your field of view by doing what is instinctive.

Setting up correctly

Slumping to pick up an object—or set up to the ball

Now, place your fist under your chin and look at the same spot on the floor. This time, you cannot drop your head because your fist is in the way. What you *can* do is bend forward at the hips and lower your eyes slightly. As humans, we find this an unnatural way to find something on the ground or watch where we step. However, for the golf setup, it is essential that we bend at the hips, thus maintaining that straight spine. This is a key element in every great setup. This is what you should learn to feel over every swing. This is also one of the few fundamentals you can improve on anytime, anywhere.

Don't allow yourself to slip back to that familiar slouch. Remember, golfers are athletes—stand like one!

Now that you understand the distinction between the slouch and an athletic posture, let's delve into the muscles used in getting set in this position. Then, we will make them stronger and more flexible, thus allowing them to repeat this position every time you set up over a ball.

Most of the muscles involved in the setup are the muscles of the trunk, called core muscles. They work with and stabilize the larger muscles in your torso, shoulders, hips, and upper legs

Flexing the knees and bowing from the hips to pick up an object or properly set up to the ball

Instinctively—and detrimentally—dropping the head to look down at the ball during setup

Bending at the hips and lowering the eyes, thereby maintaining a straight spine, for a correct setup that provide the solid foundation on which most of the golf swing is built. You need strong lower abdominal muscles to support your lower back and hips at address, and you need strong and flexible upper-back muscles to support your shoulders and arms. Your hamstrings, gluteus maximus, and gluteus minimus must be flexible to keep your lower body in the right position, and your transverse abdominis must be strong and flexible enough to support your posture throughout the swing.

The following workouts will help you stretch and strengthen the core muscles you need to make a good golf setup.

The Kitchen Chair

A

B

For this one, you need a kitchen chair or any other standard-size chair with four legs, a seat, and a back. Swivel chairs won't work, and cushy leather office chairs are not recommended. You also need a dumbbell or a medicine ball, or any object of moderate weight (between 2 and 10 pounds).

Place the weighted object upright on the seat of the chair. Then assume your golf stance at the front of the chair using the chair legs as a guide for your feet (touching the outsides of the front chair legs with your big toes should put your feet the proper distance apart).

From this position, flex your knees, bow at the waist, keep your head up, and, without moving your back, grab the weighted object as if it were a golf club (A). Now, lift the weight and touch it to the back of the chair (B), then return it to the seat.

Release, and repeat this lift until you've done it 10 to 12 times.

In addition to strengthening the front deltoids (the front of your shoulders), this exercise forces you to flex and tighten the core muscles of your abdomen and back. You have to keep your hips and legs in a good athletic posture for this lift.

As you progress in your abilities, you should add another set of 10 reps and increase the weight. I never recommend lifting more than 10 pounds in this exercise. Once you become proficient with 10 pounds of weight, you should add a third set of 10 to 12 reps.

Soccer-Ball Squeeze

For this one, you'll need a soccer ball (or a lightweight medicine ball if a soccer ball is not available) and a golf club.

Stand with your feet shoulder width apart, and place the soccer ball between your legs, just above your flexed knees. Now squeeze your legs together to hold the ball in place.

Once the ball is securely between your legs, hold a golf club horizontally across your hips by placing one hand near the grip and the other near the clubhead. From this position you should be able to bow slightly, as if you were setting up to hit a golf shot.

You should emphasize squeezing the soccer ball using pressure applied by your adductor muscles in the hip region. You will also feel pressure in your groin muscles. You should hold this position for at least 30 seconds. Once you become proficient at holding the ball between your legs and assuming the proper stance, you can repeat the exercise for a minute or more.

Two-Ball Squeeze (Advanced)

After you are comfortable with the soccer-ball squeeze, you should add a more advanced wrinkle, one that requires the addition of a tennis ball and assistance from a second person. Holding the soccer ball between your legs and the club across your hips, have a trainer place a tennis ball in the center of your back, between your shoulder blades.

Without releasing the golf club, squeeze your shoulder blades together and hold the tennis ball in place in an attempt to put pressure on the ball. Ultimately, this exercise will be most successful if you can trap the tennis ball between your shoulder blades. Hold this for 10 seconds.

This conditions you to open your chest, pull your shoulders back, and suck in your belly (a function of the transverse abdominis) while keeping your adductors, glutes, lower abdominals, and groin muscles ready for action.

If you've read and listened to golf instructors, you've probably heard of the "reverse K" position. This is how teachers describe the tilt of the upper body in which the left shoulder is higher than the right and the head is behind the ball. The analogy is that the body is contorted to look like a backward "K." I've always been dubious of this description and have found very few students who understand it. Those who do, frequently exaggerate the tilt, creating an awkward lateral spine angle and causing problems for the swing arc.

For many people the so-called reverse K position occurs naturally in gripping the golf club. Because the right hand is lower than the left, the right shoulder is naturally lower as well. However, I've also found that golfers who have weak and inflexible oblique muscles are more likely to exaggerate this tilt or contort so that the right shoulder is actually higher than the left.

The obliques, a muscle group that goes largely ignored by the general golfing public, are the muscles between your rib cage and hips on both sides of your body (the areas where love handles evolve over time). They put your shoulders and head in the proper position at address and get you poised to make a good rotation on your backswing.

Two groups of exercises, hip crossovers and oblique crunches, strengthen and stretch the obliques in ways that benefit your golf game.

Exaggerated
reverse K

Reverse K with right shoulder
higher than left

Correct reverse
K position

Hip Crossover **Stretch**

A

B

C

Lie flat on your back with your arms extended out to your sides and your knees bent so that your feet are flat on the floor (A).

Now, keeping your knees together, rotate your hips to the right while keeping your arms and shoulders on the floor and turning your head to the left (B). Hopefully you can rotate your hips and legs until your right thigh and knee touch the floor. If not, go as far as you can before bringing your legs back up and repeating the process on the left side (C).

You should do this on the left and right sides 10 to 15 times.

Hip Crossover

A

B

C

Once you can comfortably perform two sets, you should increase the intensity of this exercise by bending one knee so that your foot is flat on the floor (A). You will feel increased pressure on your lower-abdominal and hip muscles and an added degree of difficulty as you rotate your hips and legs from one side to the other (B, C).

Hip Crossover **with Physioball**
(Advanced)

A

B

C

You can add another level of difficulty by introducing a piece of equipment known as a physioball. The physioball is an inflatable exercise ball, slightly larger and stronger than a beach ball and available at most stores where sporting goods are sold.

Separate your knees, put the physioball between your legs, and lift the ball off the floor (A). You will feel a great deal of pressure in your lower abdomen, as well as in your hamstrings, your groin, and your adductor muscles.

Now rotate your hips (and the ball) to the right until your right knee touches the floor (B), and repeat on the left side (C). Be sure not to hold your breath—breathe out as you lift or lower your legs. When you can complete two sets of 10 to 15 reps at this level of intensity, you know you're getting a good core workout and strengthening the muscles needed to make a solid setup.

Oblique **Crunch**

A

B

This exercise is one of the simplest and most effective exercises for strengthening your obliques and quadratus lumborum (a deep back muscle).

Lie flat on your side with your lower arm extended in front of you and the palm of your hand on the floor (A).

Raise your torso, pulling your high shoulder toward your hip by contracting the muscles in your side (B). If you're unaccustomed to working your lateral obliques, you'll probably have trouble doing 10 to 15 reps on each side, but give it your best shot. After a few weeks, you should be able to do three sets of 20 on each side.

Oblique Crunch **with Physioball**

(Advanced)

A

B

To intensify this exercise and add a stabilizing component, try some oblique crunches on a physioball (A, B). The plia-bility of the ball increases your range of motion, while balancing on the ball requires you to focus on your core.

The biggest area of concern for golfers is the lower back. Whether you are a Tour player or a casual weekend player, strain or injuries to the lumbar region take on that "it's not *if,* it's *when*" sense of foreboding. Fred Couples's back "exploded" when he bent over to pick up a suitcase. In the 10 years since, Fred has struggled with an iffy lumbar. Davis Love found himself flat on his back in his midthirties and spent the next 5 years playing day-to-day golf depending on his twinges and pangs.

More golf-related back injuries are caused by poor posture at address than by any other source. Weak upper backs, glutes, abs, and transverse abdominis, along with tight hip flexors, put undue pressure on the lumbar region. Throw in a few thousand bad swings on the practice tee, along with a bad setup, and it's easy to see how disks and nerves are injured. Even a good setup adds pressure to your back. In summary, a golf swing is just not back-friendly even when done properly.

In a perfect setup, the left hip is slightly higher than the right, just as the left shoulder is higher than the right shoulder. From this position, the hands, arms, and shoulders are free to swing the club back on a proper plane, and the legs, hips, and torso are poised to make a solid athletic move. Many amateurs cannot set their hips in this position. They prop up on their right hips, keeping their glutes tucked and their pelvises tilted forward. This is backward, but it's common for one simple reason: Most average golfers aren't strong enough and flexible enough in their hip, thigh, hamstring, lower abdomen, and lower-back regions to set the hips properly at address. This poor setup puts additional strains on the lower back, which can lead to debilitating injuries.

In a good setup, the left hip is higher than the right

In a poor setup, the right hip is higher than the left

In reality, there is no way to prevent all injuries, especially in an area as sensitive as the lumbar region of the back, in any athletic endeavor. However, there are plenty of preventive exercises you can incorporate into your daily routines that will minimize the likelihood of injury.

The following are some of the most important exercises to protect your lower back and improve your setup.

Reverse **Crunch**

A

B

Lying on your back with your arms at your sides, lift your legs so that your lower legs are parallel to the floor and your knees form a 90-degree angle (A).

Now lift your legs and hips up toward the ceiling using the muscles of your lower abdomen (B).

This will be tough for many of you. Rarely does a golfer focus on the muscles between his navel and his groin. A few reverse crunches should help you identify the area of neglect.

Shoot for 10 to 15 reps. When this becomes easier, add additional sets until you are performing three sets of 15.

Reverse Crunch **with Physioball**

(Advanced)

A

B

To intensify and add a stabilizing component to this exercise, place the physioball between your legs and lift it and your hips off the floor (A, B). This not only works the lower abdomen, it forces you to keep the groin, glutes, adductor, abductor, and transverse abdominis muscles tight and balanced.

Back **Extension Stretch**

A

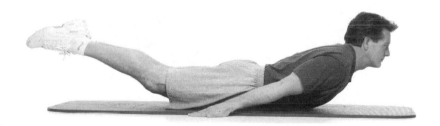

B

Lie facedown on the floor with your arms at your sides (A).

Raise your feet and shoulders off the floor as high as you can (initially, expect 6 to 10 inches), keeping your hips flat (B). This will extend your lower lumbar in the opposite direction from the normal exertion of a setup and swing. This works the glutes, hamstrings, illiacus, and psoas major (lower-back muscles) and provides balance to the abdominals. The motion will be small compared to the other exercises you've performed, but it is a vital move to strengthen your lower back. Start with a set of 10 to 15 reps, and as your fitness increases, progress until you can do three sets of 15.

Back Extension **with Physioball**

A

B

To intensify the back extension, lie with your chest and abs on the physioball, your hands behind your head, and your legs straight out behind you (A).

From this position, arch your back and raise your torso (B). You will feel the results deep in the interior of your lumbar.

Three sets of 10 to 15 should leave your back feeling fit and strong.

What to Expect

This seems like quite a workout for something as simple and innocuous as the setup. But don't be fooled: Just as a good setup is 90 percent of a good shot, these exercises are the foundation on which the rest of your game will be built. Once you work the core muscles needed for a good setup, the other fundamental positions of the swing will benefit greatly.

POSITION TWO
INITIAL TAKEAWAY

Many
teachers and players, in-
cluding greats like Hogan, Snead,
Nicklaus, Johnny Miller, and Tiger Woods,
believe that the first part of the takeaway—the
initial 18 inches to 2 feet of movement—determine
what kind of shot you are going to hit. I've never
broken out the measuring tape, but, of course, the
general idea is correct. How you begin the takeaway
determines the position at the top that is necessary
for a consistent impact position. A poor initial takeaway requires you to make a midswing correction in order to get the club back to the ball.
Sometimes, by pure luck, that's possible. Most of the time, however, it is not.

That's why I spend an inordinate amount of time working with my students on the initial takeaway.

To illustrate the importance of the first move away from the ball, think of the golf swing as a swing set on a playground. As any first grader will tell you, the most important part of getting started on the swing set is getting the seat moving in the right direction. If a kid pushes the swing a little too far to the right or the left, the seat will wobble, and it won't go very high or very fast. But if the initial motion is centered, the swing seat will track straight and fast for a thrilling ride. Your golf swing is no different. If you start the club back on the proper path, it will climb high, start back down on plane, accelerating to (and through) impact, launching the ball high, long, and straight.

Unfortunately, most new players don't pay attention to their backswings. I've heard too many students say things like "How you get it back is not important; it's how you make contact that matters." In a very limited sense (as is the case with Jim Furyk) that's true. The only moment that really matters is the millisecond when the club makes contact with the ball. Every part of the setup, positions at the top, and preimpact downswing is designed to maximize the speed and efficiency of the club. Everything after impact is a consequence of what you've done beforehand. So, if you're talented enough to preset the club at the top and hit your golf ball from a running start (like

Adam Sandler's character in *Happy Gilmore*), more power to you. Most players, including 99 percent of the players on all major Tours, aren't that coordinated.

The How and Why of the Takeaway

The sole purpose of the takeaway is to set in motion a sequence of swing events that will deliver the clubhead back to the ball, at maximum speed, with the clubface square and moving along the intended target line. Now there's a mouthful. Reams of scientific data and millions of hours on driving ranges around the world have been dedicated to the takeaway and the subsequent chain of events. Fortunately, you do not have to pioneer any of this data collection and analysis. Others have done that for you. All you have to do is follow their lead.

Great players sweep the club back, letting the core muscles, upper back, and shoulders initiate the backswing by pushing the club away from the ball. When the hands reach hip height, the shaft and left forearm form a straight line. The torso and hips have also turned slightly as the club makes its way back. This is the classic "one-piece" backswing, the one used by every successful professional and sought after by every motivated amateur.

What is a one-piece takeaway?

The terms "one-piece takeaway" and "connected backswing" have become some of golf's most-used catch phrases. Yet, like many phrases in the game ("over-the-top," "double-cross," "laid-off") they sound very golfspeak. Without knowing exactly what they mean, millions of amateurs use one or more of them every day to describe their errors *du jour*. So, let's address these positions and phrases, and we'll improve your golf *and* your golfspeak.

A true one-piece takeaway is when the club, the arms, the shoulders, and the torso all move as one piece. The upper arms stay "connected" to the body. There is no added separation between your triceps and your sides.

Here's an easy way to see and feel what that means.

Stand in the setup position and put your right hand over your heart, keeping your upper arm tucked close to your side. Point your left arm at the spot on the ground where the golf ball should be.

Now, turn your shoulders and trunk (core) 90 degrees to the right so that your left arm is pointing to an object to your immediate right. This is a one-piece takeaway. Your hands, arms, shoulders, and torso have moved together. If you can imagine making this same move with your arms extended and a golf club in your hands, you understand the principle.

To incorporate that feeling into the swing, place a towel across your chest

Getting the feel for a one-piece takeaway

and hold the ends under your armpits. Now, grip a club and try to swing. If the towel falls out, your arms have separated or "disconnected" from your body. Vijay Singh incorporates this fundamental drill in many of his daily practice routines.

Why is a one-piece takeaway important?

Knowing what one-piece takeaway means is only the first half of the equation. The second half is why a one-piece backswing is critical to your game. For this you need to go back to your imaginary swing set. Imagine how difficult it would be to swing if the forces of gravity and momentum didn't keep the chains straight. Imagine if, instead of a smooth, rhythmic flow front-to-back, up-and-down, the chains bent and the swing jerked steeply upward and came straight back down. The chaotic motion that comes as a result of this action is the same thing that happens in your golf swing when your arms and hands work independently from your shoulders and body.

Clubhead speed and consistency in your golf swing come from the same forces of momentum, gravity, and centrifugal force that you find in your

Using a towel to practice keeping the arms connected to the body

imaginary swing set. The core muscles of the body are like the steel frame of the swing, the foundation on which the motion is centered. Your arms are like the chains, performing at their peak when they are fully extended, and your hands are like the hinges holding the seat in place. Momentum and gravity will work magic at the bottom of the swing's arc if you will only allow those forces to do what they do naturally.

The first 18 to 24 inches of the backswing sets these forces into motion. If you begin the swing with an extended one-piece takeaway, initiating the motion with the core muscles, you will have to add an unwanted move into your swing to screw things up. If you start the swing with your hands and arms, leaving the core muscles of your shoulder and torso out of the equation, you will have to make several additional moves during the swing to correct this mistake. Making corrections during the 2-second span of the golf swing with the clubhead accelerating toward 100 miles an hour is no easy task. (Read: "Ain't gonna happen.") It's easier to get things right from the beginning.

Why is the one-piece takeaway so difficult?

The idea of a one-piece takeaway seems straightforward enough. You simply initiate the backswing with your large, strong core muscles rather than with the smaller muscles of your hands and arms, and you keep the upper part of your arms close to your body throughout. Ben Hogan said he felt as though his arms were bound to his torso with a strap. Tiger Woods calls the relationship between his arms and chest the magic triangle, which is just another way of describing a connected takeaway. These analogies are simple enough. So, why is the one-piece takeaway so difficult for most amateurs?

The answer comes from human nature. The only contact you have with the golf ball is through the club, and the only contact you have with the club is through your hands. It is intuitive to move the club with your hands, wrists, and arms. You have wisely bought this book, and now you are holding it in your hands, using the muscles in your wrists and forearms to hold it upright. Your hands and fingers turn the pages. If you have a drink nearby, you use those same muscles to lift it to your lips. At work, you use your hands, wrists, and forearms to type e-mails, fly airplanes, take notes, and operate machines. These are the everyday muscles of life. To ignore them in the early stages of your golf swing is just unnatural.

It's also one of the most important fundamentals in the swing. To prove it, try this simple experiment: Open your hand and slap the side of your desk, a door, or the footboard of your bed. Then, slap it again at a different angle, and again at a third. This is easy to do, because your hand and arm can move in a virtually unlimited number of directions and angles. You can even put a couple of fancy loops and swirls into your delivery as you slap your object of choice.

Now, lock your elbow against your side and slap the object again without letting your elbow and upper arm leave your body. With your elbow tucked like this, your hand comes in from the same angle every time. You have to move your body and work pretty hard to bring the hand in from a different direction.

Since golf is about consistency, wouldn't you rather have a swing that brings the club into the golf ball from the same angle every time? That is the point of the connected takeaway. Consistent and connected going back means consistent and connected down and through. Simple.

The Dreaded Reverse Pivot

Another move that prevents the amateur golfer from realizing any potential of lowering his or her handicap also occurs in the opening seconds of the swing.

Reverse pivot

Correct takeaway position

Instructors see it a hundred times a week. Afflicted students suffer its power-robbing effects without knowing how or why it happens. It is commonly known as the *reverse pivot*. In this move, the left shoulder dips, the head moves forward, and most of the player's weight shifts to the *left* (wrong) side. The arms and hands lift the club at a sharp angle. As a result, the head, body, arms, hands, and club are out of position at the top of the swing. A nearly impossible variety of midswing corrections are required to make solid contact. The outcome: a variety of ugly shots almost too numerous to list. Let's see if any of the following golfspeak sounds familiar: There's the "fat," the "thin" (which is just a few millimeters away from a "top" or, worse, a complete miss), the "snap-hook," the "weak slice," and, of course, the perennial crowd pleaser, the "S-word": the "shank."

There are plenty of causes for the reverse pivot: lifting the club with the right hand and arm, dipping the left shoulder down rather than *around* the body, and no weight transfer in the backswing, just to name a few. Surprisingly, the most common cause of these errors is poorly trained core muscles. Almost all of the ills of the reverse pivot stem from a player's attempt to initiate the swing with the small muscles of the hands and arms, while ignoring the large, strong core muscles (latissimus dorsi, pectoralis major, rectus abdominis, and the external and internal obliques).

The reason players ignore those large muscles in the golf swing is that they ignore them in their everyday lives. Imagine asking someone who sits at a desk all day to jump up and run a marathon without having trained at all. You cannot use muscles you have not developed. By ignoring the core muscles in your everyday life, you have, by default, eliminated them from your golf swing.

In other words, all the lessons you've taken and all the articles you've read about improving your ball flight are useless unless you train the core muscles to:

(a) Initiate the swing with a one-piece takeaway.

(b) Eliminate the reverse pivot.

Here are some exercises to strengthen your core muscles and train your body to start your backswing.

Chair-to-Counter **Reach**

A

B

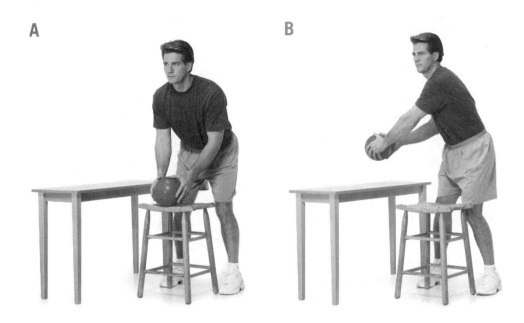

Place a chair or stool near a waist-high counter with a weighted object (preferably a medicine ball) on the seat. If you are standing in front of the chair, you should be able to touch the counter with your right hand. Now, take your stance in front of the chair, touching the two front chair legs with your big toes to ensure that your feet are shoulder width apart (A).

Keeping your feet on the floor and your arms straight, pick up the weighted object with both hands, and in one motion, turn your shoulders (B) and place it on the counter (or, if your counter is lower than waist height, as in the photos, hold the weight above it). Then return it to the seat.

You should feel this turn throughout your abdominals and in the large muscles of your upper back commonly known as the lats. After 10 to 12 reps, you will also feel it in your deltoids (shoulder muscles) and in your rotator cuff, the muscle group that gives the shoulder its rotary motion.

For optimum benefit, you should start with one set of 10 to 12 repetitions and work your way up to three sets of 15 to 20 reps.

Seated Hands-to-Floor **Reach**

Sit on the floor with your knees at a 90-degree angle so that your feet are flat. Now extend your arms in front of you, keeping your forearms raised slightly above your knees. To execute this move, lean back slightly, keeping your back straight and your arms in front of you (A).

Now, rotate your upper body to the right so your arms extend out past your right hip (B).

Come back to the starting position (C) and repeat on the left side (D).

You should feel this in your abdominals and obliques. Once you are able to perform this 10 to 12 times on each side without falling over, you should add two more sets of 10 to 15 reps.

Seated Weight-to-Floor Reach
(Advanced)

A

B

C

D

To add another level of intensity, pick up a weighted object (preferably a medicine ball weighing between 4 and 10 pounds) (A).

Keeping your arms extended and elevated slightly above your knees, rotate as before (B), return to the center (C), then rotate to the other side (D).

Do this move 10 times on each side, and add more sets as you get stronger.

Seated **Rotational Pull** (In Gym)

A

B

One of the best in-gym exercises to strengthen the muscles critical to a one-piece takeaway is the rotational pull from a seated position. This workout requires a pulley machine and a bench or physioball. Pick a resistance (weight) level you can repeat for 10 repetitions. (I recommend a starting weight of 20 to 30 pounds. These muscles are already stronger than you might think.) To start, sit on the ball or bench facing the weight so that a single pulley cable and handle is level with your chest.

Grasp the handle in both of your hands (A).

Now, without straightening your arms or letting your elbows leave your side, rotate your torso to the left, pulling the handle across your chest (B). Perform 10 reps. Then repeat on the opposite side, rotating your torso to the right. Interestingly, pulling the weights from right to left will benefit the muscle groups used to initiate the downswing, discussed later in the book. After a few weeks, you can add additional sets.

As far as square inches of muscle are concerned, the latissimus dorsi, or lat muscle, is the largest in the body. Your lats are the big muscles surrounding your shoulder blades, the ones that make bodybuilders look like they have wings and the ones that bulge in Tiger Woods's shirt when he's preparing to rip a drive down the fairway. The lats actually start on the spine in the center of your back, on your hips, and on your bottom three ribs. The fibers then twist together and attach to your humerus at the back of your armpit.

These big muscles play a huge role throughout the swing, but they're never more important than in the first 18 inches of the takeaway. By engaging the lats early, you turn your torso and harness the power of one of your body's most powerful muscles.

The most common and efficient exercise to strengthen the latissimus dorsi is the lat pull.

Lat Pull (In Gym)

A

B

For this workout, you need an overhead bar on a standard pulley or a "low-row" lat pull machine. These are standard gym apparatus that will provide the surest avenue to this particular strengthening goal. Initially, the weight used should be determined by your existing physical strength. Women should be comfortable with 20 to 40 pounds, and men should start with 60 to 80.

To execute this workout, grab the bar with an overhand grip slightly wider than shoulder width. Position yourself in front of the machine so you are facing the weight stack. Lean forward slightly with your arms extending up (A).

Slowly and smoothly pull the bar down toward your thighs, squeezing your shoulder blades as close together as you can (B). After a brief pause, slowly raise the bar to the starting position. Two sets of 8 to 10 reps will be a solid workout. Add weight as you get stronger.

For a consistent proper, connected takeaway, the shoulders and back muscles (deltoids) must be not only stronger but also very flexible. Previous exercises have focused on strengthening. Now, let's stretch the same muscle groups.

Overhead **Shoulder Stretch**

A

B

Using your driver (or a stretching bar in a gym), grasp both ends of the club, held horizontally in front of you (A).

Slowly raise both arms, keeping your elbows locked (or as close to locked as you can) until the driver is directly over your head (B).

Here's where it gets harder. See how far over, then behind, your head you can move the club without your elbows bending (C,

C

D

D). Most men lack range of motion just past vertical, due primarily to inflexible rotator cuff muscles.

Interestingly, many if not most PGA players can do this with ease. It is an integral part of their warmup stretching. It is important to *slowly* add to your range of motion and keep proper form (firm elbows). Start with about 10 repititions, though the number of reps in this drill are not as important as working toward, and just past, your previous flexibility limits.

Overhead Shoulder Stretch
with Weight

A B C

To add another level of intensity and combine this stretch with a light strengthening exercise, repeat the previous overhead stretch with a lightly weighted bar (5 to 10 pounds) or dumbbells. This will allow you to continue your range-of-motion training with a rotator cuff workout (A, B, C). A side benefit is that, without even thinking about it, you have continued to open up the chest muscles, helping with your shoulders-back, chin-out setup posture. Once again, 10 to 15 reps will get you started.

Few people know what the deltoids are. Fewer still know that each deltoid has three distinct parts—a front, middle, and rear. Associated with the deltoid is the rotator cuff, consisting of four different muscles: the supraspinatus, infraspinatus, teres minor, and subscapularis. The golf swing requires you to work all of these muscles, which presents a problem for many amateurs. While you might think your shoulders are strong—you don't have any trouble lifting a box of sweaters over your head and placing it on the closet shelf—you have no idea how your front deltoid balances with your middle and rear deltoids. It is not necessary to understand these muscles in detail; you need to know only that, to hit a golf ball harder, you must make them stronger.

For these reasons, you need to expand your shoulder exercises to work all three areas of the deltoid and every rotational muscle in the rotator cuff. One of the best exercises to coordinate the motions of the middle deltoid with the trapezius (the muscle that runs from your neck to your shoulder) and the rhomboid (the central back muscle that's underneath the trapezius) is known in the gym as a *fly*.

Bent-Waist Fly Stretch

Stand with your knees flexed and your feet apart, then bow at the waist with your back straight until your torso is almost parallel to the floor. Allow your arms to hang down, palms facing each other.

Grasping imaginary weights, raise your arms straight out to the sides, as shown,

until they just pass shoulder height. You should feel tension across your upper back and the tops of your shoulders. This is predominantly a stretch, but it will prepare you for a more advanced, strengthening version later. Accomplish 10 to 15 reps.

Bent-Waist Fly **with Resistance**

A

B

Repeat the bent-waist fly with an elastic resistance band, available at any sporting goods store. Stepping on the center section of the band with both feet, grasp the handles (A). Raise your hands to shoulder height (B). Your upper-back and shoulder muscles will have to work fairly hard to overcome the elasticity of the band. This is a particularly useful workout because the elastic resistance bands are easily transportable, making it a favorite of mine while traveling. They are also common equipment in any fitness center. Three sets of 10 to 15 reps is a wonderful workout for your upper back.

Bent-Waist Fly **with Weights**

(Advanced)

A

B

The ultimate evolution of this exercise uses dumbbells (A, B). The exercise is performed the same as with the elastic resistance band, except free weights are substituted. Obviously, unless you spend a good deal of time working out with free weights, I would recommend starting with light weight, 5 to 7 pounds, for three sets of 10 to 12 reps.

What to Expect

So, will these regimens exorcize all the demons from your takeaway and backswing? Well, in a word, yes. With the proper takeaway path *and* these exercises, you will look like a Tour player, at least for the first 18 inches of the swing. Additionally, you will have made a great start for the rest of your swing. You still need to visit the driving range and work on making a solid, one-piece takeaway. What these workouts absolutely will do is prepare your body for what lies ahead on the range. Your instructor's advice about the backswing will be a lot easier to implement once you've conditioned your body to make the right first moves.

POSITION THREE

TOP OF THE BACKSWING

How
does Charles Howell III,
whose 5-foot-11 frame barely tips
the scales at 155 pounds, consistently
launch tee shots more than 300 yards? Where,
in this marathon-runner's physique, does this
fantastic clubhead speed come from? What secret
powers does he possess? More important, what can
average golfers do to generate that same power and
still stay perfectly balanced?

Much of the answer lies in the third fundamental
position: the top of the backswing.

In speaking with my students, I like to
compare the top of the backswing to
a locked and loaded catapult
or the flexed

limbs of an archer's bow at full draw. Enormous energy is harnessed in the taut, "loaded" parts of these machines. Once released, the arm of the catapult or bow unleashes that stored energy, firing the projectile toward the target. As any Roman centurion could tell you (had he not been dead for hundreds of years), the catapult gets its range from the length and coil of the arm. The longer the arm, the farther the projectile flies. It's simple physics. (Is there such a thing?)

Michelle Wie's backswing

Stuart Franklin/Getty Images

The same principle applies in golf. The golfer with the longest extension and greatest coil at the top of the backswing will usually hit the ball farther than anyone else in his group, even if that golfer looks more like Charles Howell than like Arnold Schwarzenegger. You see this in golf every day.

It is not reasonable to consider teenage sensation Michelle Wie physically stronger than NFL Hall of Fame running back Emmitt Smith. But Michelle can fly her tee shots every bit as far as Emmitt's best drive. She can do this thanks to the tremendous extension and coil she creates on her backswing. Emmitt's arms bend (shortening the distance between his hands and his torso—what we will later refer to as width), and his shoulders don't coil as far as they should. So he loses potential power and, thus, clubhead speed and distance. Sure, Emmitt is immeasurably stronger than a teenage girl, but because he fails to get into an extended, coiled position at the top of his backswing, he simply cannot accelerate the clubhead as consistently as Michelle Wie does.

What Is Width?

"Width" and "extension" are two more of those well-worn buzzwords in golf. Rarely does a Sunday telecast go by that some network golf analyst doesn't comment on the great extension or width so-and-so is getting on his backswing. "Look at the width he's creating. That's why he's hitting it so long off the tee today, Johnny." Unfortunately, too few of those analysts explain what "width" means in context.

Width refers to the distance between the hands and the torso during the backswing. Extension of the arms, away from the torso, is how we achieve the width. For the most part, we can use these expressions interchangeably.

The farther away from the ball your hands are at the top, the more leverage you have, and the more clubhead speed you're likely to generate on the way down. Think of your catapult again. If the arm is 20 feet long, it generates more speed at the moment of release than would a 10-foot arm. A player who has a straight left arm, a full shoulder turn, and good weight shift will create the greatest distance possible between his hands and the ball at the top of the backswing. That's good width.

The player who breaks down his left elbow, fails to turn his shoulders fully, and doesn't transfer his weight to his right side shortens the distance between his hands and the ball. This puts him at a disadvantage when it comes to generating clubhead speed. With the same effort, the player who has created more width will almost always hit the ball farther than the person who has gotten "short" on the takeaway.

How about Coil?

Jack Nicklaus used to describe his backswing as a spring. At the top, Jack said, he felt as if someone had wound the top portion of a spring while holding the bottom portion steady, creating torque and building energy. As old-school as that analogy is, it's still accurate. At the top of the backswing, your shoulders and torso have coiled around a flexed but firm right leg much like Jack's spring analogy.

Some teachers refer to this as loading the right side, while others preach the "X factor," which is the ratio of shoulder turn to hip turn. I prefer to keep things simple. Your right leg and hip are the anchors of the backswing. Your shoulders, arms, and torso coil against that steady base, creating the same kind of torque Jack talked about 30 years ago. This builds a storehouse of energy for you to unleash on the downswing.

Coil is what separates the great players from the beginners, or even from the average weekend players. If you look at the backswing of a truly accomplished player, you will see shoulders turned more than 90 degrees, with the right leg and right hip acting as a brace for this coil. The turn is so full that the end of the left shoulder is completely underneath, or even past, the chin. (Tiger Woods's shoulder turn can extend even beyond this point.) In fact,

Good width on the takeaway

Narrow width on the takeaway

this degree of shoulder turn has linked all of the players ever counted among the game's greats.

This is the ultimate power position in golf. It is what allows Tour players to hit mammoth drives that seem to defy the laws of physics. Failure to achieve this position is what inhibits amateurs from hitting it longer. A full coil of the shoulders, a steady right leg and hip, and great extension on the backswing are the keys to hitting the ball 20, 30, even 50 yards farther.

Unfortunately, most amateurs focus on how far they're taking the club back as opposed to how far they are turning their shoulders. Again, I'll use my friend, Emmitt Smith, as an example. During

one of my first lessons with Emmitt, I put a towel under both of his arms and told him to swing without the towel falling out (see page 50). After a few failed attempts, Emmitt finally got the towel to stay in place by making a hip-high swing. "I'm barely taking it back," he said.

"Right," I said. "That's because you're turning your shoulders only a few degrees. The rest of your backswing is a lift with your hands and arms, which is the kiss of death."

"Why?" he asked.

I thought about my answer for a second, and then asked, "How many autographs do you sign in a year?"

He looked confused, but said, "I don't know, thousands."

Andrew Redington/Getty Images

Tiger Woods's backswing

Jamie Squire/Getty Images

Vijay Singh's backswing

David Cannon/Getty Images

Jack Nicklaus's backswing

Bob Gomel/Time Life Pictures/Getty Images

Arnold Palmer's backswing

TOP OF THE BACKSWING

"Exactly," I said. "But your signature is different almost every time. Sure, it looks the same, but there are always subtle differences. If you overlaid a dozen of your signatures, you probably wouldn't find two that are identical. If you can't consistently repeat something you do with your hands as often as signing your name, how do you plan to consistently repeat a golf swing using your hands and arms?"

The lightbulb came on, but, still, Emmitt's mind was writing checks his swing couldn't cash. "I can't play golf with a backswing this short," he said.

"You want to take it back farther?"

"Of course," he said.

So, I grabbed his shoulders and twisted him into a full turn. I can't remember the exact words he used after this revelation, but I know they were unprintable.

"That's how you make a full backswing," I said.

Unfortunately, I can't jump from these pages and turn your shoulders into the proper position. What I can do—and later in this chapter will do—is suggest some exercises that will help you with a more pronounced rotation of your shoulders and upper torso, as well as the subtle rotation of your head.

Head Rotation

Go back to the Tour players' pictures on page 71 and look at their heads. All the great players have their heads po-sitioned well behind the ball during their backswings, to give their shoulders room to turn. You can see this if you draw an imaginary line from their noses to the ground. In every case, the head is rotated so that the player's nose is pointed well behind his right foot. This subtle move frees up the shoulders to turn fully around the right leg and hip.

How the head rotates depends on the player. Vijay Singh and Jack Nicklaus set their heads to the right before the swing as part of their preshot routine. Sam Snead rotated his head and kicked in his right knee as a trigger to begin the backswing. Tiger, Arnold, and Tom Watson rotate their heads during the backswing. Ben Hogan and Bob Jones did this as well. Even players who are known for "looking up" during their downswings, like Annika Sorenstam and David Duval, rotate their heads slightly to the right during the takeaway.

This move is small but critical. If a player's nose is pointed at the ball, the shoulders can't fully turn and weight can't shift to the right side. The head impedes the takeaway, which can lead to a short backswing, or, even worse, a reverse pivot.

Proper rotation of the head doesn't appear to be difficult, but it is. Once again, this is an unnatural move that must be practiced time and time again until it is conditioned into your swing. The reason rotating the head is so tough is that most right-handed people are also right-eye dominant. (Lefties tend to be left-eye dominant.) It's unnatural and difficult to turn your dominant eye away from something you are trying to hit.

If you don't believe it, rotate your head to the right, close your right eye, and try reading the rest of this page.

While this demonstration is not as physically demanding as some of the other exercises in this book, by the time you get to the last line on this page, you'll see how unnatural this feels.

Now, set up as if you are about to hit a golf ball, rotate your head, close your

Rotating the head for a full shoulder turn at the top of the backswing

Failure to rotate the head, resulting in a reverse pivot

TOP OF THE BACKSWING

right eye, and take the club to the top of your backswing. This will feel awkward at first, but you will be aware of your head's slight rotation (to the right) at the top of the swing.

Once you feel comfortable taking practice swings with your head turned and your right eye closed, put a patch over your right eye and try hitting a few balls. At first you will stick the club in the ground behind the ball. You might shank a few as well. But once you become accustomed to looking at the ball through your left eye, rotating your dominant eye away from the ball will come much easier.

Wearing an eye patch to get used to rotating your dominant eye away from the ball

Chair-Turn **Stretch**

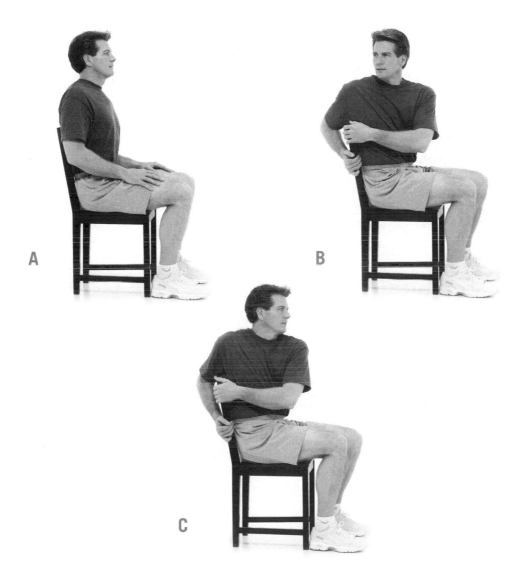

A

B

C

To get the feel of what a full shoulder rotation feels like, sit upright in a straight-backed chair with your back straight and your feet on the floor, shoulder width apart (A).

Now, turn your upper body to the right so that you can grab the back of the chair with both hands (B). You should do this without coming out of the seat or letting your feet leave the floor.

From this position, rotate your head back to the front to increase the intensity of the rotation (C).

Hold your body in this position for 30 seconds and repeat on the left side.

Left-Hand Handshake **Stretch**

A

B

You can practice this reach and stretch virtually every day. With the assistance of a friend, coworker, or any waist-high, fixed handle, this will help you visualize and execute a more full rotation.

First, from a normal golf setup (gripping an imaginary club), place your right hand on your right hip. Rotate your trunk and shoulders in a one-piece takeaway (as discussed in the previous chapter), and with your left hand, slightly exaggerate a reach to your partner (or a fixed handle) standing to your right. Have the partner provide some resistance, pulling your left hand away from your trunk, thus extending the width we talked about earlier (A). Hold for 30 seconds.

When this is properly done, your shoulders and upper trunk will be rotated a full 90 degrees and your left arm will be fully extended. With a club in your hand, you would be in a perfect takeaway position (B).

The previous two moves are designed to condition your body to the static position you want to achieve extending toward the top of the backswing. But nothing about the golf swing is static. The next exercise will give you a sense of the motion required in a full shoulder turn.

Medicine Ball **Rotation**

A   B

C

Sit on the floor with your legs extended in front of you, and pick up your medicine ball (A).

Rotate your shoulders and torso to the left (B).

Now, rotate your shoulders and torso in the opposite direction (C). Complete this process 10 times to strengthen and stretch the muscles required for a full, powerful upper body rotation. Once you are comfortable with this exercise, you can add additional sets of 10 to 15, with a maximum of three sets per workout.

Step and Reach

A

B

Stand upright with your feet together and your arms at your sides (A).

Step to your left while rotating your upper body, turning your head to the left, and raising your arms toward the sky (B).

Now bring your arms back down, step back to the center, and repeat with the right foot, rotating to the right and reaching for the sky again. In addition to giving you a sense of the weight shift in the golf swing,

this conditions your body to combine the turn with the full extension of the arms.

Okay, most of you won't earn a spot in Twyla Tharp's dance company, but if you incorporate this reach-and-stretch movement into your top-of-the-backswing workout, you will improve your takeaway and add distance to your golf shots. Do it 5 to 10 times, or until you have thoroughly embarrassed yourself.

Step and Reach
with Medicine Ball (Advanced)

A

B

C

To add intensity to the step-and-reach movement, perform it while holding a medicine ball (A, B, C). In addition to adding weight, the medicine ball forces you to co- ordinate your arms and hands so that they work as a single unit, just as they should in the golf swing.

Kneeling **Rotational Pull** (In Gym)

A

B

This is a great gym exercise for the extension and coil of your backswing. Attach a handle to a pulley cable and add a light-to-moderate weight or band resistance. Kneel on your right knee, but keep your left leg up so that your left knee forms a 90-degree angle, your left foot is flat on the floor, and your upper leg is pointed toward the machine. After kneeling, position the pulley at chest height and take the handle in both hands (A).

Turn your shoulders and torso 90 degrees (or more) to the left (B). *Hold this position.*

The resistance felt in holding this position is the goal of this workout. Now, rotate your shoulders back to the starting position. You should perform 10 to 12 reps of this exercise from each side, with emphasis to the right for right-handed players.

This isn't about how many pounds you can lift; it is about increasing strength in the rotational muscles in your shoulders and arms, critical to a strong position at the top.

Swing with Left Foot
on Medicine Ball

To put an exclamation point on the hard work you've done to build a solid backswing, pick up a club, place your left foot on the medicine ball, and take a full backswing. The medicine ball should stay put, but you should have no trouble making a full, coiled turn while keeping your right leg steady. This is what loading the right side feels like. With the proper training, it's the feeling you will get every time you take the club back. Do this drill 5 to 8 times.

Touch and Toss

A

B

This one requires the help of a trainer, workout partner, or friend standing two or three paces away, depending on the weight of the ball. Stand with your feet slightly wider than shoulder width apart, holding a medicine ball in both hands (A).

Rotate to your right, and, keeping your head high and back straight, bend at the knees and hips (B) and extend the ball to the outside of your right foot.

Now, push your body up and to the left as you rotate your torso so that you can throw the medicine ball to your trainer standing behind your left shoulder (C). Hopefully, your trainer will catch the ball (don't throw it at someone who isn't looking) and toss it

C

back to you. Do this for a minimum of 10 reps. Change sides and begin again, squatting to the left and tossing the ball behind your right shoulder.

Your heart will be pounding when you finish this, but you will also be training your body to load and shift your weight as you make a full backswing.

What to Expect

Once you've trained your body to make a fully coiled, connected backswing with great extension (width) around a solid right-leg-right-hip foundation, you've put yourself in position to hit the ball farther and straighter than you ever have in your life. Now, you have to deliver the clubhead back to the ball. So, let's get to it.

POSITION FOUR

INITIAL DOWNSWING

Everything
you've done so far—the
setup, the connected initial takeaway,
the coiled and fully extended backswing—
has been designed to build and store energy.
Now it's time to unleash that energy, time for the
swing to change directions, for the club to start on its
downward path back to the ball, and for your body to
maximize all its speed and efficiency in preparation for
the moment of truth: the instant that club meets ball.
Different players have different ideas about how to
initiate the downswing. Ben Hogan said the hips
start the downswing by turning to the left,
which pulls the arms to an inside
plane while creating speed
and weight

transfer. He believed you couldn't turn your hips too fast on the downswing. Tiger Woods, who swings the club faster than Hogan could have ever dreamed, says he likes to start the downswing by "shifting my weight easily back to the left side, and then letting the arms fall downward in front of my chest. I don't want my shoulders unwinding so fast that they get way ahead of my arms." Tom Weiskopf, who had the most beautiful swing in golf in the 1970s, said he started the downswing by moving his left knee toward the target, while Steve Elkington, the active player who has held the "best swing in golf" title says: "During the first critical moment of the downswing, the club has to go into freefall. The key is to get the feeling of pushing your weight straight down into both feet. This allows the shoulders to unwind a little bit, while balancing you enough to make a powerful turn through the ball." Sixty years ago, the greatest amateur who ever lived, Bob Jones, said: "The hips lead as the unwinding begins, and by pulling against the hands and the weight of the club, draw the left arm taut." Jack Nicklaus, holder of 18 professional major trophies, dropped his left heel to the ground and turned his left hip out of the way when starting his downswing. Greg Norman initiated his weight shift and hip turn by driving off his right leg.

All these feelings are different, and all of them are correct. If you surveyed 50 of the top players in the world, you'd probably get 20 different answers on how to initiate the downswing. None is better or worse than the other. For the best players in the world, the answer to what starts the downswing is "whatever works."

In 1922, the great Harry Vardon wrote one of the most concise passages on this subject. According to Vardon, "During my first tour of the United States, when the game was young in America, there were many theories among the spectators as to how the shots were accomplished. I remember being cornered by a man who, just after I had made a rather good shot, jumped the ropes and asked excitedly of a friend beside me: 'Which arm did he do that with?' My companion put the question to me, and I had to look for a moment to make sure that one arm had not become shorter or longer than the other. I do not believe there is such a thing as a 'master arm' in the real golf swing. The two arms work as one and as part of the entire mechanism of the body. . . . It is fallacy to suppose that any particular part of the body, such as the arms or wrists, has to be very specially applied to the task of hitting the ball. The whole anatomy should work as one piece of mechanism, with the club as part and parcel of the human frame."

Vardon had it right: The whole body contributes to the backswing; it makes sense that the whole body should deliver the club back to the ball.

If you've done everything correctly on the backswing, your left arm is extended, your shoulders are fully turned, your right leg and hip are steady, your head has rotated behind the ball, and your spine angle has remained steady. Your abs are tight, the muscles of your back are engaged, and you feel a springlike tension in your hip flexors, groin, and glutes. From this position, you are ready to uncoil and unleash all the power you've built up.

Letting the Legs Lead

While many great golfers have different feelings on the downswing, all have one thing in common: They all transition to the downswing by moving their lower bodies. In every great golf swing the legs and hips move first. The torso follows the hips; the shoulders follow the torso; the arms follow the shoulders; the hands follow the arms; and the club follows the hands. That's the order of the downswing.

Another way to think of it: The sequence is from the ground up. The hips rotate to the left, and the weight shifts from the right to left side. This action, initiated with the large muscles of the legs, glutes, and lower abs, is like the handle of a bullwhip being thrust outward. The action doesn't seem particularly fast or powerful, especially when viewed in comparison with the rest of the swing. However, just as the seem-

ingly slow movement of the whip handle creates great speed at the whip's end, so too does the movement of the legs and hips on the initial downswing generate great speed at the end of the club.

Far be it from me to disagree with Hogan or Bobby Jones, but I have a slightly different take on the relationship between the hips and shoulders. Hogan, Jones, Sam Snead, and countless others said they felt as though the hips "pulled" the shoulders and club down. This makes some sense. If you fold your arms across your chest, make a full shoulder turn, and rotate and shift your hips to the left, the shoulders naturally follow. But to say that the hips pull the shoulders into place implies that the shoulders cannot swing without the legs. That's simply not so.

I can hit very good golf shots from my knees. Jim Flick, one of the best instructors of his generation, can hit perfect tee shots while sitting in a chair. From these positions, the hips and legs aren't doing much, yet Jim and I can still hit the ball well enough to make our point. How is that possible? And how does it square with what the greatest golfers of all time say about the initial move on the downswing?

The lower and upper body have to be synchronized.

You can't hit the ball well without turning your shoulders and torso on both the backswing and the downswing. But the turn back to the ball on the downswing is made much more powerful and effective by engaging the lower body. When the hips lead, the right shoulder, the hands, and the club drop slightly, putting you in the perfect position to deliver the club to the ball with maximum speed. Sure, I can turn my shoulders and swing the club from a kneeling position, but I cannot generate anywhere near the clubhead speed that I have when I've engaged my legs and hips.

As we have discussed earlier, clubhead speed is ball speed, which is distance. It becomes obvious, then, that real power comes from engaging the lower body, not from strong arms or an overly developed chest. This proves Harry Vardon's point: The hips and legs really are important, but so are the shoulders, arms, and hands. No one single body part controls the golf swing.

The hips don't pull the shoulders into position as much as the rotation of the hips and shifting of the weight from right to left assists the shoulders and arms in getting the club into the right spot. This hip-leading motion isn't unique to golf. Barry Bonds's first move when going after a fastball is a hip rotation, but that doesn't mean Barry's shoulders are subservient to the movement of his hips. His swing is synchronized—legs, hips, torso, shoulders, arms, and finally hands—so that his entire body contributes to the homerun swing. You see the same thing when Andy Roddick and Serena Williams blast ground strokes in tennis. The hips lead, followed by the torso, shoulders, arms, and hands. In the swings of all great ball-and-stick (or racquet) athletes, the hands lag behind the larger body parts, and the stick, bat, or racquet lags the hands. The sequence is the same. Even though they are the only contact the athlete has with his racquet, bat, or club, the hands are always the final element in the complicated chain reaction of the swing.

Strong hips and stabilizers create strong downswings.

Amateurs have a hard time leaving their hands out of the downswing. One of the most common swing-killing moves comes when an average golfer gets his initial downswing sequence out of order and starts the club down with his arms and hands. This is commonly called *casting*, because the move looks more suited to bass fishing than to golf. When the hands start the downswing, the right shoulder comes up and out toward the ball, the head dips, and the spine angle becomes rounded. Rather than the hands and club dropping behind the player's shoulders, they outpace the shoulders and hips back to the ball. As a result, the energy stored in the flexed shaft is spent early in the downswing. There is a loss of clubhead speed and path control at contact.

It takes a lot of coordination to make contact once you've cast the club with your hands. For those talented few who actually make reasonable contact, the result is a weak slice or a head-high pull—neither shot landing anywhere near the intended target.

Even pros occasionally let their hands outpace their bodies. If you ever hear a Tour player say he "got ahead of it" with his hands or "fanned it," he's talking about this hands-first move on the initial downswing.

Fixing this move isn't easy. Most prominent golf magazines have built their circulations for 50 years on the promise of curing your slice. "Fix Your Slice" is and always will be the mainstay of golf magazine tips. Why? Simple. The cast (outside-to-in) slice move is *easier for the untrained body to do.* Why is the slice the predominant ball flight of 90-plus percent of beginners and unmotivated amateurs? The reason has always been that an on-plane, inside-to-out swing path is less intuitive and more difficult to train the body to execute. When was the last time that you saw a Saturday morning infomercial like: "Buy my new Turbo-Graphite-Mega-Blah, Blah Blaster, and try *my* clinically proven methods, and I'll help you get rid of that pesky high, long draw *forever.*"

As long as there are new golfers, there will be an endless supply of tip-givers, quick-fix ads, and undecipherable nonsense about changing this weak ball flight.

There is one and only one proven way to cure a slice. The body must be trained to put the club on the correct path, in spite of the natural tendencies to do otherwise. Most amateurs who are serious about the game understand what they *should* do; they just can't do it.

Cindy's initial downswing

Barry Bonds's batting swing

Serena Williams's forehand

Brad Mangin/MLB Photos via Getty Images

Richard Drew/AP Worldwide

Casting the club on the downswing

Unlike the pros, amateurs have not placed sufficient emphasis on training core muscles to turn the hips and transfer the weight. The few that have done this may not have the stabilizing strength to support the rapid unwinding of the shoulders.

Casting the club doesn't come from a lack of knowledge or a lack of coordination. It comes from a lack of strength and flexibility to create this rotation consistently. Hogan was able to fire his hips as fast as possible because he had the torso strength of a horse. Steve

Elkington can feel like he's "driving his feet into the ground" on the downswing because his stabilizing core muscles keep his spine angle steady as he makes that move. Most amateurs attempting either of those moves for the first time may be somewhat discouraged by their inability to make square contact. Even after these concepts sink in a bit, it's all too easy to slip back to the old slice swing path once we've taken our new swing to the golf course. We simply cannot allow the poorly trained muscles to take over our swings again.

You can, indeed, cure your slice forever. To do so does not require buying a new titanium driver or subscribing to 12 issues of a glossy magazine. What it does require is a commitment to strengthen and stretch your hips, glutes, groin, and stabilizers. There is work to be done, but it is doable. If you want to add distance to your drives and eliminate the dreaded "banana ball" from your inventory, here are some sweat-equity moves to get your body ready.

Door Frame **Pull Stretch**

A

B

Set up in front of an open door frame or next to another vertical support without a club in your hands (A).

Make a full backswing, reach back, and grab the support with both hands. Now, try to rotate your hips and shift your weight, even though your grip on the support will preclude such a motion (B).

This is an isometric exercise that strengthens the muscles in your back, sides, shoulders, hips, and glutes. (For you

first-year med students, these are your left latissimus dorsi, teres major, infraspinatus, middle and lower trapezius, and rhomboid, as well as your gluteus maximus, gluteus medius, iliacus, and psoas major.)

To achieve maximum benefit from this exercise, hold it for 20 seconds, take a 10-second break, and then hold it for another 20 seconds. Now, repeat this on the opposite side, rotating your shoulders to the left and holding the other side of the door frame.

Standing Rotational **Pull**

A

B

In the gym, attach a rope handle to a high pulley cable, add a moderate amount of weight or resistance, and then stand with your feet shoulder width apart and your right side facing the weight stack. Turn your shoulders, reach up, and grab the handle with both hands (A). Now, rotate your hips and shoulders to the left, pulling the handle down in front of your body (B). Slowly return the handle by rotating your shoulders and torso to the right. Do not move your feet when executing this.

This strengthens the core rotational muscles of your hips, torso, and arms. You should perform 10 to 12 reps on each side, and then add more sets of 10 to 15 reps as you become stronger.

The pillar muscles are the stabilizing muscles of the shoulders, core, and hips that allow you to maintain a solid posture and consistent spine angle throughout the swing. It is critical that these muscles be strong and taut during the initial downswing, the time when many amateurs lunge downward with their arms and hands, destroying all semblance of good posture. To improve your pillar stability, perform the following two exercises.

Pillar Stabilizer **Pushup**

A

B

Lie facedown in a modified pushup position with your forearms resting on the floor and your elbows forming a 90-degree angle. Your body should be straight, supported by your forearms and toes (A). Hold this position for 20 seconds.

Once you are comfortable holding this position, you should add more intensity by rocking your body forward until your chest touches your arms (B). Then return to the original position. Keep your torso off the floor, and do three sets of 10 to 12 reps.

Pillar **Rotation**

A

B

C

Start from the same position as the pillar stabilizer drill (prone and supported by your forearms and toes) (A).

Slowly rotate your hips as far as you can in one direction (B), then the other (C). Do not let your hips touch the floor. Your back should remain straight and your chest high as you rotate your hips. Five reps in each direction is a good workout.

This combines the pillar stabilizing strength you need with the hip rotational movement you use to initiate the downswing.

To balance your front and back stabilizer muscles you also need to strengthen your sides. These are the muscles that keep your upper body angled properly throughout the swing and allow your shoulders, arms, hands, and club to fall into position after your hips rotate at the start of the downswing. Here's an exercise to strengthen your side stabilizers.

Side Stabilizer Hip Lift

A

B

For this workout you should lie on your left side and prop up on your left elbow. Point your left arm in front of your body, and keep your elbow directly below your shoulder. Only your left hip and left leg should be touching the floor (A).

Now lift your hip off the floor until your body is straight (B). Hold your body in this position for 20 seconds, then slowly lower your hip to the floor, and repeat. You should hold yourself up for three 20-second lifts on your left and then your right side.

The following exercises will help increase the strength of your quadriceps (the large muscles in the fronts of your thighs) and glutes, two muscle groups that are integral to initiating the downswing.

Physio **Squat**

A

B

To strengthen the glutes and quadriceps, stand so that a physioball is trapped between your lower back and a wall. Keep your hands on your hips and your feet shoulder width apart (A).

Bend your knees and squat until your knees form a 90-degree angle and the ball is between your shoulder blades (B). Make sure your feet are far enough in front of you

that your knees don't pass your toes. Now return to your start position and repeat 10 times. If a physioball is not available, simply "sitting" against a wall, with your thighs parallel to the floor, will replicate this exercise.

Once you are comfortable performing one set of 10 reps, add two additional sets of 10 to 15 reps.

Physio Squat
with Medicine Ball (Advanced)

A   B

To reach another level of intensity while adding a groin workout, do the physio squats while holding a medicine ball between your thighs, just above your knees (A, B). This will require you to focus on the muscles along the inner portion of your thighs (adductor), as well as the quads and glutes.

One set of 10 to 15 reps is a workout. When you can do three sets of 15 to 20 reps, you're becoming a first-rate athlete.

The next series of exercises will work all of the muscles you should use to initiate your downswing: glutes, hip flexors, quads, and abs.

Front **Lunge**

A

B

From a standing position (A), take one large lunge step forward with your right leg (B). Now, bend your right knee to 90 degrees and drop your left knee toward the floor. Maintain a straight back throughout the exercise. Repeat until you have completed 10 lunges with each leg. You can choose to do all 10 reps with one leg, then switch, or alternate legs after each rep.

Front Lunge **with Golf Club**

(Advanced)

A   B

For a higher degree of difficulty and addition flexibility training, hold a golf club horizontally in front of you at the start of the lunge (A). As you drop one knee toward the floor, simultaneously raise the club up and over your head (B). As you straighten up from the lunge, return the club to chest height. This will reinforce the shoulder stretching discussed in the Top of the Backswing chapter, and add an element of balance, necessary to all good swings.

Front Lunge **with Medicine Ball**
(Advanced)

A

B

For additional intensity, replace the golf club with a weighted medicine ball and repeat the front lunge a minimum of 10 times with each leg (A, B). The additional weight will give your shoulders a workout while forcing you to focus on your balance and posture.

In addition to being one of the best workouts for stretching the hip flexors, glutes, abs, back, and shoulders, the following move simulates the rotational moves of the downswing.

Back Rotational Lunge
with Golf Club

A

B

From a standing position, hold a golf club horizontally, waist high (A).

Step back with your right leg and bend your left leg until the knee is at a 90-degree angle and the right knee is close to the floor (B). After you have lowered into the lunge,

pause, and rotate your torso 90 degrees to the left.

Repeat this with the opposite leg, rotating your torso in the other direction. Complete 20 of these lunges, 10 in each direction.

The previous exercises have worked on your strength and flexibility in the hips, glutes, abs, back, and shoulders, the areas you need to be strong and flexible as you begin your downswing. These next concepts will work on your explosiveness. Some of these are high-impact and highly aerobic. If you fatigue, or if you feel pain in your joints, stop immediately, take a break, and resume at a less intense pace. *These should all be considered advanced moves.* You will not have compromised the intent of this chapter if you choose not to perform all of these exercises.

Rotating Jump (Advanced)

A   B

Place two golf clubs on the ground to form a cross. Now place your left foot in the upper left quadrant. Place your right foot in the lower right quadrant, keeping your upper body still and facing straight ahead. Place your hands on your hips (A).

From here, bend your knees, pause (keeping your weight on the balls of your feet), then jump, rotating your hips slightly while you're in the air (B) so that you come down with your left foot in the lower left quadrant and your right foot is in the upper

right quadrant. This "hop-scotching" drill returns to the original foot position every other jump. Repeat this as many times as you can in 1 minute. Speed and explosiveness are the keys to this one. Rotate your hips as quickly and efficiently as you can, counting the number of times you can jump and twist in 60 seconds. As you progress with this, attempt to deepen your knee bend and add explosiveness to each jump (jump higher and with added intensity).

Lateral Leap
with Medicine Ball (Advanced)

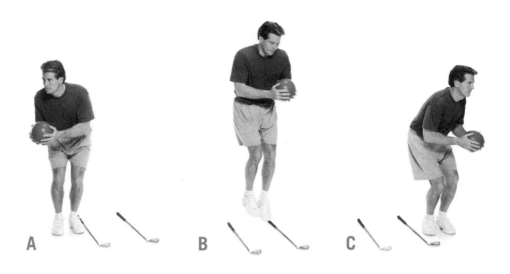

A   B   C

During the initial downswing, your hips not only rotate but also shift from right to left, building momentum down the target line. To get this sense of both lateral and rotational movement, place two clubs on the ground, parallel to each other, approximately 2 feet apart. Now stand to the right of the clubs (A) and face straight ahead, while holding a medicine ball in front of your abdomen.

From this position, flex your knees, and leap laterally across the golf clubs (B).

When your feet land, pause, and rotate your torso 90 degrees to the left (C) After this extension, pull the ball back to your abdomen, then rotate back to a position facing forward (just as you began). Now, leap back across the clubs, rotating your upper body so that when your feet land, you can extend your arms and the ball to the right.

Repeat this exercise as many times as you can in 1 minute. This one will get your heart pumping. It will also condition your body to make the proper lateral and rotational moves during the downswing.

Explosive **Step** (Advanced)

A   B

To train your body for an explosive initial move, place your left foot on a 1- to 2-foot step (A), and drive through your quad and glute, propelling your body up. You might not get more than a couple of inches off the step, but that's okay. It's the explosive action that matters.

While pushing off with your right leg, keep your right leg straight and extend it behind you, squeezing your glute while using the leg for balance. You should also extend your arms up and over your head as you jump (B).

You must keep your knee flexed, your back straight, and your upper body leaning slightly forward when you land, the same position you want to maintain throughout your golf swing.

Do as many reps as you can on your left leg in 30 seconds. Then switch to your right leg and repeat as many times as possible for another 30 seconds. This is another one that will get your heart rate up while fatiguing your glutes and quads. If you can't make it for the full 30 seconds on each leg, perform as many as possible in 15 seconds, and work your way up.

Explosive Step
with Medicine Ball (Advanced)

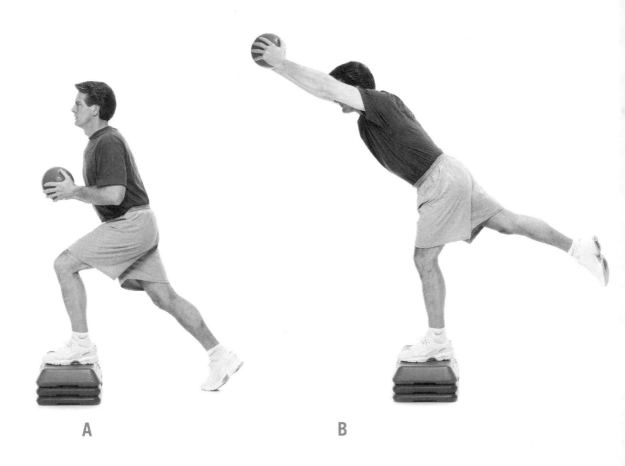

A

B

For one of the most intense workouts of your life, try the explosive step drill while raising a weighted medicine ball over your head (A, B). Not only will this add weight to your jump, you will also have to adjust your balance during the exercise.

What to Expect

The preceding workouts have focused on rotational flexibility and strength in your core muscles and legs, which drive your torso around and through the impact area. Developing these muscle groups will help you maintain an on-plane downswing, critical to avoiding the dreaded outside-to-in casting move.

Strengthening these muscles for the downswing is no easy task. The payoff, however, is measurable. How much would you give to hit the ball farther *and* cure your slice for good? If an hour of sweat a day is among your answers, you should have no trouble.

POSITION FIVE

IMPACT

It
all comes down to this.
Everything you've ever done in
golf—the equipment you've bought, the
lessons you've taken, the green fees you've
paid, the swing changes you've made, the drills
you've worked on, the swing thoughts you've im-
planted in your noggin, the waggles and twitches of
the preshot routine you've mastered, your setup, your
takeaway, and your downswing—has been in antici-
pation of this decisive moment. This is the millisecond when clubhead meets ball, and your
talent, ability, and efforts are laid bare for
all to see. The ball flight will be the report card for every minute of
"school" you

have attended to improve your game.

Jim Colbert, a 28-time winner on the PGA Tour and Champions Tour, calls impact "the great truth teller." According to Colbert, "You can dress the part, act the part, go through the motions, but the moment the club meets the ball, all the BS is out the door."

Colbert is exactly right. Unlike a lot of life's activities, golf provides instant and irrefutable feedback. If you swing the club correctly, the clubhead will strike the ball at the proper angle, with enough speed to send the ball soaring toward your intended target. The ball flies straight because the clubface is pointing toward the target and the path of the swing moves along the target line. A slice (the ball curving to the right) occurs when the clubface is pointing right of the target or the club's path imparts clockwise spin on the ball. A hook comes from the clubface pointing left and a path that imparts a counterclockwise spin.

All of those things happen in a tiny fraction of a second, the only moment in golf that counts. Everything before impact has been to prepare you for this instant, as well as the extension and finish, after the ball is on its way. So why have I spent so much time getting you to this moment? Why do so few instructors focus on impact? Why worry about your setup or your backswing? The reason the pre-impact and post-impact portions of the swing are important, and the reason nobody in the game has an impact coach, is simple: A

driver's clubhead is moving at around 100 miles an hour (or faster) when it makes contact with the ball. Impact lasts under a hundredth of a second. Once the club has started down, with the clubhead accelerating toward the ball, virtually no one who plays the game can make a conscious decision to change or improve the swing path or clubhead angle. All you can do is make the right moves ahead of time to get the club in the proper spot at impact.

What Happens at Impact

The physics of impact are straightforward. The coiling action of the backswing and uncoiling action of the initial downswing create centrifugal force, much like a track and field athlete tossing a discus or hammer. The straight left arm follows the lead of the hips and shoulders and pulls the club toward the ball. Your hips have rotated to the left, and your weight continues to shift down the target line, while your shoulders rotate into a position similar to your setup. Meanwhile, two critical hinges formed by the folded right elbow and cocked right wrist unhinge at the bottom of the swing's arc *at the last possible moment,* unleashing the swing's afterburners and generating tremendous speed. The clubhead will still be accelerating as it passes "through" the ball.

Are you lost yet? If not, you're in the minority.

The mechanics of what happens at impact make for great 19th-hole discussions. But, from a practical standpoint, understanding the physics of the club's exterior circular motion in relation to the ball's linear force won't shave a single stroke off your score. You need to know what you should *feel* at impact, and what motions you can work on to improve your chances of making solid, high-speed contact.

What Should You Feel?

Hogan said that at impact he felt as though he were hitting the ball as hard as he could with the palm of his right hand, but not so hard that the right hand overtook the left. Bob Toski, the leading money-winner on Tour in 1954 and the godfather of modern golf schools, said he felt like the club was swinging his body through impact and that his arms were chasing after the ball. The late Davis Love, Jr., winner of 14 professional events and a world-class teacher (whose most famous pupil shares his name), said he felt as if his arms got 6 inches longer at impact. Byron Nelson, winner of 11 consecutive PGA Tour events (not to mention 18 events in 1945 alone), said he felt as if his straight left arm was leading the club through the ball while his head remained steadily positioned over his right knee.

There are hundreds of possible feelings at impact. The best one is the one

Standing tall and swinging long
through impact

Lunging during impact

that works for you. Nobody knows what a good shot feels like better than the person who hits it. I tell the majority of my students to feel as if they are "standing tall and swinging long" through impact. That advice comes from many years of watching amateurs lunge at the ball, dropping their heads and folding their left arms as if they're chopping firewood or driving a pickax into the ground. I understand this lunging motion. The ball is on the ground, and you're trying to hit it, so every instinct in your body is telling you to dip your head and shoulders as you throw the club down.

By telling my students to stand tall, what I'm really saying is "Don't change your spine angle." Your torso and head should remain on the same horizontal plane through impact that you've maintained throughout your swing. No dipping or lunging.

When I say, "swing long," I'm telling my students to extend their arms through the hitting area. Bobby Jones knew this as well as anyone. In describing his feelings at impact, Jones said, "The straight left arm, the immoveable head, and the action of the right shoulder and right arm hold the player down to the ball until it has been started away."

Staying long and tall through impact puts you in the positions Jones described, and the positions every great player in history has tried to emulate.

What Does "Releasing the Club" Mean?

Back in the 1970s, when he was the most recognized golf instructor in America, Bob Toski was teaching a golf school when one of his students said, "Bob, I've heard all these great players talk about releasing the club at the ball. What exactly does that mean?"

Toski pounced. "You want to know what releasing the golf club means?" he said.

The student and many of his colleagues nodded.

"Okay, I'll show you." Toski picked up the student's 7 iron, took a swing with it, and threw the club about 20 yards down range where it stuck in the mud like a javelin. "That," Toski shouted, "is what releasing the golf club means."

Shtick aside, "releasing the club" is golfspeak that a lot of players use, but few understand.

"Release" in golf refers to the point when the club catches up with the hands, and the hands catch up to the arms. This occurs when the right elbow straightens and the right wrist returns to a neutral position, the position you had at address. This is when the levers of the right elbow and wrist release their energy and the club travels its fastest. Hopefully this happens at the moment of impact.

To understand the release, think about Derek Jeter snagging a ground ball and making a throw to first. When set to throw, his shoulders lead his arms, and his right elbow comes into his side just before he extends his throwing arm toward first base.

This is the same motion that occurs in the golf swing. The hips have turned to the left (some players call this motion clearing the hips), the shoulders have turned back to the same position that they were in at address, and the bent right elbow has dropped toward the right hip before the right arm straightens.

Watch slow-motion footage of Derek at the plate, swinging at a fast ball. In the hitting zone, his right forearm catches, rolls over, then passes his left

Bobby Jones at impact

Ben Hogan at impact

wrist. This is the release point, at which the bat speed is the highest.

If Derek's throwing arm outpaces his body, the ball will miss the target. If he adds tension in his throwing hand and arm, he will lose velocity. And if he dips or lunges, the ball could go anywhere.

The same is true of your golf swing. Releasing the club is not about hitting the ball as hard as you can with one particular hand or about pulling the club with one arm. It is about releasing the energy that you have built up in one consistent, powerful blow. The moment of truth. *Impact.*

Muscling Through Impact

"Just what muscles are the key players at impact?" you may ask. This is an excellent question and rarely addressed in the discussion of swing fundamentals. The muscles you've already begun strengthening in your sides, back, and shoulders are now contributing to more acceleration and more clubhead speed. The larger muscles in your legs (hamstrings and quads) and the obliques in your sides are helping drive your torso and shoulders around and

Robert Laberge/Getty Images

Vijay Singh at impact

Stuart Franklin/Getty Images

Karrie Webb at impact

through the hitting area. Where we have not focused is on the very same muscles that we did *not* want you to emphasize in the initial takeaway—specifically, the hands, wrists, forearms, and arms.

The biceps and triceps play a key role in delivering the club back to the ball, a fact that is lost on many players, even some of the best in the world.

One of the trainers at my gym also trains David Eger, a two-time Walker Cup player and winner on the Champions Tour. "David doesn't be-

lieve in working his triceps," she told me. "He says you don't need them for golf."

I was stunned. "Of course you need them," I said. "What muscle does he think straightens his right arm through impact?"

David is a great player, so I feel comfortable picking on him. But he's not the only Tour player with some misguided notions on the physiology of the swing. When he arrived on Tour in the 1950s, Gary Player was seen as a

Throwing a golf ball to practice a release, with the right elbow moving close to the right hip, the hips and shoulders turning to the left, and the right arm straightening

zealot for lifting weights. Harry Vardon once put forth that the golfer's muscles should be long and supple, because short and hardened muscles, like a boxer's, would restrict quickness and flexibility at the instant of impact. He, like Player, was ahead of his time.

As late as the 1980s, pros thought that swimming ruined your golf swing. Today we realize that swinging in a swimming pool is a wonderful concept that will help you recognize the processes leading up to impact. If you have access to a pool, submerse yourself so that only your head is above water. Now take an old club and make some half-swings. The club will come out of the water, but your hands should not. The water's resistance will strengthen and stretch every muscle you use in delivering the club to the ball. It will also keep your posture tall. Just as your natural instincts urge you to lunge at the ball when it's on the ground, those same instincts will scream for you to keep your head above water. Swinging in a pool reverse-wires your logic. Instead of telling you to dip your head and throw the club at the ball, your instincts will now tell you to keep your head up and your back straight. After 30 or 40 slow-motion swings, you will know what a long and tall golf swing feels like. If you can try this routine periodically, the concept of "tall, yet solid" will become evident. This drill is yet another example of how fitness in golf has come a long way.

One fitness trait that is now recognized as common to all great golfers is stronger-than-normal hands and wrists. In the impact zone, a stronger release of the hands can be accomplished with a few simple exercises. These include wrist rolling, curling, and rotating, as described on the following pages. (More advanced impact exercises, discussed later, are best accomplished in a gym.)

Wrist **Club Lift**

A

B

Here's one you can do every day in your office. Standing, hold a golf club in your right hand just as you would if you were standing behind the ball picking your target line in your preshot routine. The clubhead should be resting on the floor in front of you, and your thumb should be on top of the grip, just as it would be if you were preparing to take a normal, two-handed grip (A).

From here, keep your arm at your side, but lift the clubhead as high as you can by bending your *wrist only* up toward your shoulder (B). This will probably be a small move. Most of you won't be able to lift the club parallel to the ground. But keep working. Lift and lower the club 15 to 20 times with each hand, trying to get the clubhead higher each time.

You will feel this in the flexor and extensor muscles of the forearm. These are the muscles that hinge and release the wrist during the swing. The stronger you make them, the more likely you are to control and accelerate the club through impact.

Wrist **Roll**

A

B

Another basic wrist-strengthening exercise involves a rolling motion, grasping a broom handle or lightweight bar with hands about a foot apart. Slowly roll the handle (with an overhand grip) in one direction, focusing on maintaining muscle tension in the wrists and forearms (A).

Try a progressively harder variation by adding a 3- to 5-foot length of twine or thin rope, secured at one end to the middle of the handle. To the other end of the rope, attach a light weight, such as a 5-pound barbell weight. Now, repeat this rolling motion, winding the rope up and around the handle (B). Just a small amount of weight significantly increases the effort to roll the handle. After you have completely wound the rope up, *slowly* roll it in the opposite direction, unwinding it back to the rope's full length. Use 8 to 10 reps to get started. Your forearms and wrists will definitely let you know they have just discovered a whole new torture.

Wrist **Curl**

A   B

Holding a light weight, place the back of your forearms, palms up, on a hard, flat surface, such that your hand hangs off an edge, allowing freedom of movement up and down. You can even use your upper leg, with your hand and wrist extending past your knee (A). Slowly curl your wrist and hand up and down, through its full range of motion (B). To make this a bit more effective, allow the weight to roll down toward your fingertips as your wrist flexes downward, then curl the weight back upward. Do this with both overhand and underhand grips, 8 to 10 reps with each grip.

Wrist **Rotation**

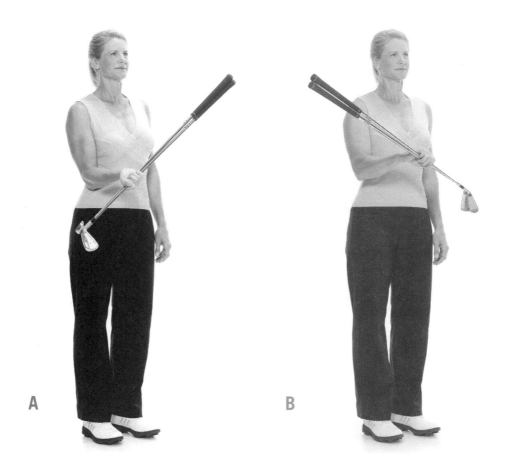

A

B

Slowly rotate your wrist and the clubs fully in one direction, then back the opposite way. The length of the clubs will resist this rotation and will increase strength and flexibility. Do 8 to 10 reps with each hand.

Now that your hands and wrists are on their way to being stronger, how can you simultaneously work all the muscle groups we've been discussing? You need to focus your newly found strength to the bottom of the swing, to achieve maximum club-head speed and control at impact.

Situp Toss

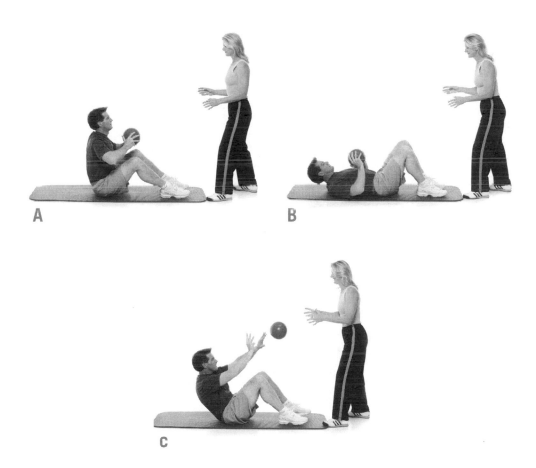

Sitting on the floor with your knees high and your feet flat, hold a medicine ball against your chest with both hands. Ask your trainer to stand directly in front of you (A).

Lean back, stopping at the lowest point from which you can still pull yourself back up to a seated position. For some of you this will be a small move, only a few degrees. Others will be able to touch your shoulder blades to the floor (B). The important thing is to recline as far as you can and bring yourself back up quickly.

As you pull up to a seated position, toss the ball to your trainer (C). Then have your trainer pass it back. When you catch it, initiate your recline. Do this 10 times. As your motion gets stronger, use a more explosive toss, adding velocity and intensity.

A golf club's weight (and to a far lesser extent, its wind drag) provides a resistance to the muscles used to swing it. The energy expended in swinging a club is substantial. After a few dozen swings, anyone who is not in Golf Shape will begin to fatigue the muscles specific to the swing. Wouldn't it be helpful to have stengthening workouts that use all or part of an actual swing motion? Here are two of my favorites for focusing power and increasing your clubhead speed in the impact zone.

Weighted **Driver**

A

B

The advantages of swinging a weighted club have been understood for decades. What is frequently overlooked is the fact that there's no need to go to a golf superstore to purchase the latest, greatest infomercial product. A properly weighted club can be found right in your own home. Just tie a simple 18- to 20-inch hand towel in a knot around a driver shaft and let the knot slip down to the clubhead (A). In your first swing, you will realize what an elegant solution this really is. You will have added both weight and wind resistance to the swing, while maintaining the natural feel of the club (an advantage lacking in most purchased training aids).

C

While focusing on hitting all seven of the fundamental positions, concentrate on the muscles in play as you execute the downswing (B, C). You will definitely feel the resistance in your left-side muscle groups.

An added benefit to the weighted clubhead is that the centrifugal force of the weight helps your extension in the takeaway and your full rotation during the follow-through (more on that later). I recommend 15 to 20 swings, very slowly at first. By the 12th to 15th swing, you should be swinging with more authority. Repeat this at home or in the office three times a day. In time, you can add a second towel. Your clubhead speed with your normal driver will begin to increase almost immediately.

Crossover **Cable Pull** (In Gym)

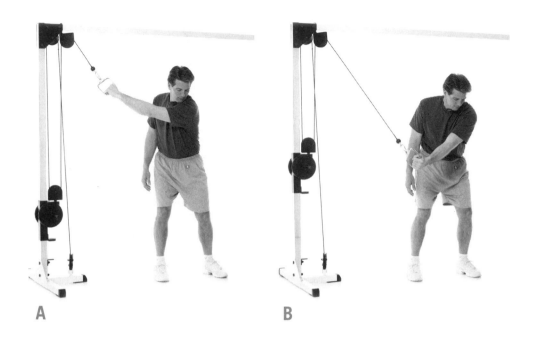

A   B

This workout requires the use of a cable apparatus found in every gym. It uses pulley weight as resistance against most of the muscles used to begin the downswing. Since your left arm and side are pivotal in the downswing (for you right-handers), using your left hand and side to perform this exercise will quickly pay dividends.

Adjust a pulley to head height and attach a handle. Standing 3 to 4 feet from the pulley, face it and then turn 90 degrees to the left. Reach up and across your body with your left hand and grasp the handle (A). This position should approximate where your left hand is just after you've initiated the downswing.

Adjust your standing position accordingly, with your weight biased on your right side. With a light weight on the pulley (5 to 10 pounds to start), slowly and methodically pull the handle down and across your body in the same path your left hand travels on

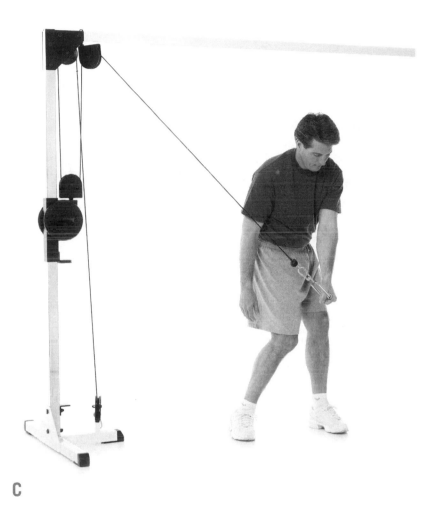

C

the downswing (B). You will feel resistance in the left side of your back and in your left triceps, forearm, and shoulder. As this simulated swing progresses, your right leg will meet resistance as it drives your hips in their rotational path around to the left. Finally, the range of this pull stops as your left arm straightens, almost exactly where your left hand is in the impact zone (C). Your weight will be on your left side, and your hips will

have cleared to the left. Do this for 10 reps, adjusting your setup to achieve the simulated downswing. Then change position to do 10 reps with your right arm. In time, more weight can be added.

This will absolutely strengthen the muscles critical to the downswing and add a higher level of intensity to the weighted driver workout.

Your hamstrings work in tandem with your glutes to keep your lower body level while your hips rotate through the hitting area. This last impact-specific exercise develops strength in your hamstrings.

Leg Curl

A

B

Lie facedown on the floor with your arms by your head and a medicine ball between your feet (A).

Now squeeze the ball between your feet, lift, and pull it toward your glutes by bending at the knees (B). Keep your torso and hips on the floor as you bring the ball up and then return it to the floor. Try three sets of 10 reps initially. It may be awkward to add a heavier medicine ball as you get stronger. Instead, add repetitions and slow down the entire movement to add intensity.

What to Expect

Pros make hitting the golf ball look easy because they use all the appropriate muscles of the body to generate consistent clubhead speed. Their motions look effortless and their power limitless because their bodies have been trained to create maximum acceleration at the millisecond the club passes "through" the ball. At other points, their swings might appear fluid, "oily," even lazy. But don't be fooled. Every Tour player on every Tour in the world has trained his or her tail off to groove a repeating swing, for that moment when club compresses and launches the ball. This millisecond is all that really separates the beginner from Tiger Woods. That, and a few hundred million bucks, earned by the perfection of a marvelous swing.

You can do the same (except the millions of bucks part). All it takes is training. A few weeks of working on the regimens in these chapters, and you will be hitting the ball farther and more consistently than you ever dreamed—or at the very least, much farther than you are now.

POSITION SIX
EXTENSION

Davis
Love III tells a great story
about extension in the follow-
through. He was talking to Byron Nelson
when, as often happens in such discussions, the
subject of Nelson's 11 consecutive wins came up.
"Did you have one swing thought that carried you
through that streak?" Davis asked.
"I had two thoughts," Nelson said. "The first was the
ranch I wanted to buy. I needed to earn $20,000 so I
could buy it. I thought about that a lot. My second
thought was to keep the back of my left hand
moving toward the target as long as I could
after hitting the ball."
Davis waited for the rest of
the lesson but

realized Nelson had no intention of going further. "That's it?" Love asked. "That's all you thought about?"

"That's all," Nelson said. "It seems to have worked."

Indeed it did. Nelson's streak is considered the greatest record in professional sports, and the one least likely to be broken. To me, it was somewhat puzzling that the one swing thought Nelson focused on throughout the longest winning streak in golf history concerned where his hands were *after* the ball was on its way. He won 11 consecutive tournaments thinking about his hand position post-impact!?

Why did it matter where Nelson's hands were after he hit the ball? Once contact had been made, the ball was on its way. He could have let go of the club and thrown it down the fairway after impact, and it wouldn't have changed the outcome of the shot. So, why did one of the greatest players in history, the man credited with creating what we call the modern golf swing, focus so intently on a part of the swing that had nothing to do with hitting the ball?

The answer is simple: Extension after impact, or, thinking about the position of the hands, arms and body after impact, affects how the club hits the ball.

"Autopilot" at Impact

Ted Williams, the greatest hitter in baseball, was asked what he thought about when he was hitting the ball. "Nothing," Williams said. "I don't know anybody who can think and hit at the same time."

Ted's pearl of wisdom applies to golf. As I've said before, at impact the club is moving at 100 miles an hour. Some Tour players swing the club at 120-plus. Initial velocity of a Men's Tour player's ball leaving the tee is between 160 and 190 miles an hour, depending on clubhead speed and how squarely the club makes contact. *It is impossible to manipulate the angle or path of the clubface at that speed.* In fact, your brain can't send signals and have your hands respond fast enough to change *anything* at the moment of impact. Most pros, and virtually every good instructor, will tell you that a *single swing thought* just prior to the takeaway is all they can manage. Once the swing is initiated, putting the club in the seven key positions (most important, the impact and extension) is accomplished entirely on "autopilot." You cannot "think" the club to the ball. Proper extension, in reality, started before the swing even began.

The reason Byron Nelson thought about extending the back of his left hand down the target line after impact is because that thought put his hands in the right position at impact. Byron correctly recognized that his brain-to-hand reaction time wasn't quick enough for him to think about impact. In order to control the club's path through the hitting area, he had to think about where his hands would be after the ball was on its way. After years of practice, these thoughts translated to his swing dynamics.

This is true for amateurs as well. To control the path of the club at impact, you need to think about the path the club travels after the ball is long gone. To control the angle of descent at impact, you have to think about the position of your hands in the opening moments of the follow-through. And in order for you to square the clubface at the millisecond when club meets ball, you have to think about where the club should be in the milliseconds immediately following impact. But let me emphasize this again: *All* of this information must have been processed by your brain, and under control of your "autopilot," long before the swing actually began.

What Is Extension?

In the context of the post-impact golf swing (as opposed to our "extension/width" discussions earlier), the word *extension* refers to the straightening of the right arm and the continuation of the club along the target line after the ball is on its way. It's called extension because both arms are fully extended in the initial follow-through. Then the left arm begins to fold and the right arm remains straight as the club continues in its elliptical path around the body. By the time the club is hip high on the follow-through, the right arm and club should form a straight line that points directly at the target.

Extending the club down the target line is important because the path of the club after impact mirrors the path before impact. If you point the club at the target in the moments immediately following impact, you've probably delivered the club to the ball along that same path. Furthermore, this emphasis on extension has guaranteed that the club is still accelerating when the ball gets in the way at impact.

Byron Nelson immediately after impact

It's also important, as Byron Nelson pointed out, that the back of your left hand move toward the target. This is not because your hands magically control the flight of the ball after it has left the clubface or because you want to look good for the cameras. You think about the back of your left hand moving down the target line because such a swing thought keeps your left wrist from collapsing before impact.

If you've played golf for any length of time, you've probably heard someone described as being a "handsey" player or someone who "slaps at the ball" with the hands. These are descriptions

The back of the left hand moving down the target line, keeping the left wrist from collapsing

of a golf swing where the trailing hand overtakes the lead hand before impact. The handsey golfer cups (or "breaks") his left wrist before the club meets the ball, thus changing the moment when the clubface rolls from open to closed. If this move is timed *perfectly*, the ball will fly straight. But the odds of repeating this slapping action are only slightly greater than those of winning the Powerball jackpot.

By thinking about the back of your left hand moving down the target line, you eliminate the temptation to slap at the ball, and you improve your chances of hitting a quality shot.

The milliseconds immediately following impact should mirror the first second of the initial takeaway. While on the takeaway the left arm remained straight and the shoulders rotated to the right, after impact the right arm remains straight and the shoulders rotate to the left. Because of this mirroring, many of the exercises you performed in the Initial Takeaway chapter apply here. Take a few moments to review them. See which ones you had trouble with, and work on those again. I'm not suggesting you double your workout, but it is crucial that you spend adequate time on the initial takeaway drills since they apply to your initial follow-through as well.

The rest of the chapter presents some additional exercises unique to the post-impact position of the swing. They are complementary to your initial takeaway workouts and will yield dramatic improvements in how squarely the clubface contacts the ball ("solid" in golfspeak), and how efficiently you accelerate the clubhead through the hitting area.

Swing a Broom
to a Waist-High Finish

A

B

Grip a broom near the end of the handle and make a full swing (A), but instead of following through completely, cut off the follow-through when the handle reaches hip height (B). Because it is longer and heavier than your longest club and the bristles oppose the air, the broom offers a great deal of resistance as you swing.

Finishing your full swing with a waist-high follow-through forces you to focus on extending your arms and the broom down the target line. If you make 30 of these swings, you will feel the extension in your forearms, shoulders, and back.

Extend the Shaft Up the Left Side

A   B   C   D

Immediately after swinging the broom to a waist-high finish, pick up a golf club and choke down on the shaft so that you are gripping the club just a few inches from the head. Holding the club here means the grip and shaft will have to extend up the left side of your rib cage (A).

Now take a full swing at a reduced speed. More than likely, the shaft will slap your left rib cage with some authority (B, C). This is what happens when your hands rotate too quickly through the impact area and you fail to get good extension on the initial follow-through.

By slightly delaying your release and extending just a bit farther, the shaft will not

hit your ribs at all (D), regardless of how hard you swing. This will be tough, but you should follow your 30 swings with the broom with 20 of these swings. This is a bit of a conditioned-response move. Your muscles will be fatigued from swinging the broom, so your natural inclination will be to get lazy and throw the club with your hands at the bottom of the swing arc. If you do not focus on delaying the release, you'll be nursing bruises along your rib cage for a few days.

The combination of the broom swing and this extended-shaft drill will train your mind and body to keep your left hand and arm moving down the target line while your right arm releases and extends the club.

One of the things that make it difficult to extend the club, hands, and arms through the hitting area is a lack of strength in the core muscles used to properly rotate. Unlike in the backswing, where the turning motion is slow and deliberate, the rotational move through impact and extension is at full speed. This kind of explosive rotation of the torso requires active and strong stabilizer and abdominal muscles. Here are some exercises to engage and strengthen those muscles.

Bicycle

A

B

Sit on the floor with your knees bent at a 90-degree angle and your feet suspended a few inches off the surface. Now lean your torso back so that you are balancing on the upper portion of your butt. Your back should remain straight and your head up. You can stabilize yourself by putting your hands on the floor—your abdominal muscles will not have to work as hard to balance you.

Holding this position may be torturous at first. If that's the case, hold it as long as you can. Work on this every day until you can hold the position for 20 to 30 seconds.

Once you can hold that posture for 30 seconds, extend your arms out in front of you (A). Now, rotate your torso to the left while extending your right leg. Then pull the right leg back and straighten the left leg as you rotate to the right (B).

Start with 10 reps on each side (for a total of 20) and work up from there. Once you can complete 15 reps on each side, you can feel confident that your stabilizer and rotational muscles are toned and ready for the follow-through.

Bicycle with Medicine Ball
(Advanced)

A

B

To add a higher degree of intensity to the bicycle, hold a medicine ball in front of your chest (A). Repeat the pedaling move from the previous drill. The weight of the ball will increase the difficulty of the torso rotation. You can hold the ball level with each rotation (B) or, if this becomes easy for you, touch it to the floor as far as you can reach to the side.

Do this for 10 reps on each side. Make sure the moves are quick. This is an explosive exercise. Once you can touch the medicine ball to the floor, push your torso up and around while pedaling your legs as quickly as you can. This will give you the feeling of rotating your body at full speed as you do in the golf swing.

Right after impact, the hips continue to rotate to the left, which means the left knee moves to the left and the right heel comes off the ground. Some players, like Greg Norman, begin the hip rotation and weight shift by pushing off with the right foot. Others feel the sensation of the left hip turning. Either way, the calf muscles play a crucial role in the weight shift and hip rotation. Here's a move to strengthen your calves while working on your explosiveness.

Toe **Raise**

A   B

Stand on a step so that your heels hang off the back and your weight is balanced on the balls of your feet. Slowly lower your heels an inch or two below the level of the step (A). Then fire your calf muscles and rise up onto your toes as quickly as possible (B).

Do this a minimum of 15 times. You will feel it in the back of your lower legs—the gastrocnemius and soleus muscles, as well as in the Achilles tendons just above your heels.

The final two exercises for the extension work the abductor muscles (outer thighs) and adductor muscles (inner thighs), respectively.

Abductor Lift

A

B

Lie on your side, resting your head on your lower arm (A), and raise your upper leg as fast and far as you can without bending at the knee (B). Perform this motion 10 to 15 times on each side.

Adductor Lift

A

B

While still lying on your side, bend your top leg until you can put your foot flat on the floor in front of you (A). Now lift your lower leg as fast and far as you can by squeezing the long muscles along the inner portion of your thigh (B). Do 10 to 15 reps on each side.

What to Expect

Don't let anybody fool you into believing that the way you finish your swing is irrelevant. The motions you make immediately after impact are a direct result of all the preceding positions. In golf, function follows form. A tall, on-balance finish is highly unlikely without solid fundamentals to get you there. Working through these exercises will improve your extension. Your new ball flight will help prove my point.

POSITION SEVEN
FINISH

An
accomplished young player
asked me an interesting question
recently. We had just spent 20 minutes
working on the finish to her swing. Hot and
tired, she took a water break and said to me, "Why
are we spending so much time on the follow-through?
The ball is already long gone at that point."
Of course, in a limited sense, she was right. The finish
has no direct effect on the shot. By the time you reach
the pinnacle of your follow-through, the ball is
yards away, and the outcome of the shot has
been determined. There's nothing a pretty
finish will do to improve a poor shot;
however, an ugly finish rarely
follows a good

shot. For a quality teaching pro, the finish provides forensic feedback on the good and bad parts of your swing. By watching the finish, he or she can tell how the ball flew even without having watched it leave the clubhead.

In the previous chapter's discussion about Byron Nelson's hands just after impact, I strongly emphasized how important proper extension is through the hitting area. One cannot consciously manipulate the hands in the impact zone to correct an improper path. But concentration on proper extension helps ensure proper clubhead path and acceleration as the head passes "through" the ball. Now, let's advance this concept to the completion of the swing.

If you maintain your spine angle through impact, you should be standing tall at the finish. If you shift your weight properly from the top of the backswing through impact and extension, 90-plus percent of your weight should be on your left side. And if you extend your hands and arms properly through impact, your hands will finish over your left shoulder, and the toe of the club will be pointed at the ground when the swing is complete. As my student aptly pointed out, none of these positions affect the shot. But they do provide a critical tracking mechanism for the swing you just completed.

"Thinking about being in the right position at the finish puts you in the right positions earlier in your swing," I said to my student. "That's why you

work on it. I couldn't care less what you look like after the ball leaves, except for the fact that your finish is a road map of your swing. If you've done everything correctly, you should end up in a good position at the finish." (I tell my more advanced players this: "One way to remind yourself to finish tall and on balance is to imagine you are playing in the Pro-Am at Pebble Beach and the TV cameras are on you!")

"So, if I think about finishing in the right spot . . . " my student said.

"You have a better chance of doing the right things earlier in your swing" was my reply.

Finish Tall

One of the biggest follow-through mistakes I see among amateurs is what I call the hang-back finish. This is when the back is curved and the right shoulder dips low on the follow-through. The hands are too high (usually over the player's head) and too much weight hangs back on the right side. This can result from a number of mishaps, including the hands outpacing the shoulders and arms on the downswing, and inadequate rotation of the hips.

Most players who suffer this malady hit ugly hooks. (Is there another kind?) These shots barely get more than head-high and dive quickly to the left. Because the weight never transfers to the left side, and the hands and arms outpace the core, the clubface rotates shut before impact. Other names for this horrific ball flight (frequently preceded by an expletive) include duck hook, snipe, hoover, smother, and the ever-popular snap hook that Ben Hogan once described as "the terror of the field mice." As Lee Trevino accurately pointed out, "You can talk to a fade, but a hook just won't listen."

One of the first pieces of advice I give to students suffering from the smother is to stand tall through impact. In fact, I often tell them to try to intentionally "top" the ball and to finish almost completely erect. This always earns me some skeptical looks. How, my students wonder, could the follow-through cause a duck hook? The answer is: It can't. But by thinking about standing tall on the finish, you are more likely to stand tall at impact, keeping your right shoulder high, turning your hips, and shifting your weight to the left side.

Standing tall and swinging long through impact is easy for me to say but not so easy for my students to do. In addition to the body's innate desire to lunge at an object sitting on the ground, you need long and strong core muscles to keep the head and torso on a consistent plane. A current student of mine, a low-handicapper, can generate tremendous clubhead speed with very consistent contact, but when he misses, it's a big, big hook. I can tell, just by watching his finish, whether his ball was a long, high draw in play, or a never-gonna-be-in-the-fairway hook. His finish will telegraph his results virtually every time.

Finish on Balance

The other critical component of the finish is your balance. There is no more telltale sign of a bad golf swing than the awkward little dance a player goes through on the follow-through to keep from falling over. I've seen players who finish with both feet facing the hole, wondering why the ball hasn't flown directly to the target. The variety of these little gyrations is endless.

A balanced swing leads to a balanced finish. The weight shifts to the right side at the top of the swing, down the target line during the swing, and onto the left side at the finish. Rocking back on the right foot, falling forward onto your toes, and moving your feet to catch yourself at the finish are all signs of a swing that has thrown you out of balance.

The most common culprit in the off-balance swing is the dreaded lunge. Throwing the club at the ball with the hands and arms and dipping your head and torso during the downswing alters your center of gravity when the club is at peak speed and the forces of gravity and centrifugal force are at their highest. Any change in your spine angle throws off your balance at this critical moment in the swing.

Another contributor is the natural instinct to try to "scoop" the ball into the air. Since the ball is on the ground, and your goal is to get it airborne, every synapse in your brain is telling you to lift, scoop, and hang back on your right foot. To understand this predilection, take a simple test: From a setup position, hold a golf ball in your right hand, turn to the top of your backswing, and try to throw the ball underhanded straight up in the air. To do this you probably shifted your head and weight to the right as you brought your arm down and tossed the ball up. Your brain has correctly commanded your body how to toss the ball.

Hanging back at impact   Hanging back at finish

Those same impulses are disastrous in your golf swing. For starters, you aren't trying to throw the ball into the air. The loft of the clubface and the backspin you impart on the ball (by hitting down and through it) launches the ball into the air. Any attempt to lift or scoop the ball has the opposite effect. The clubhead will strike the ball with an upward, glancing blow, leading to a top or a low, thin slice. You also cut the distance of your shot significantly by shifting your weight and momentum *away* from the target, instead of toward it. This is the equivalent of telling Barry Bonds to stand at the plate on his front foot only. It's possible that Barry will get a hit or two from this position, but the home run spigot will be shut off for good.

Standing tall at impact

Standing tall at finish

FINISH

Finish on Plane

If, at the top of the backswing, you could draw a line in the air along your club's shaft, the shaft should pass through that same line on the follow-through. When this happens, you know that the core muscles of your torso, hips, and shoulders have been the central power plant of the golf swing. If your club finishes on a higher line (or plane) than it passed on the backswing, your arms and hands must have manipulated the club at some point during the down-swing. If you finish on a lower plane than the one you found on your backswing, your right arm and shoulder must have overpowered and outraced your hips, shoulders, and firm left side.

In a perfect finish, your left elbow bends and stays close to your left side, and your right arm straightens and carries the club around your body and over your left shoulder. This is a mirror image of the club and arm positions at the top of the backswing.

The plane of the club shaft at the top of the backswing should be reflected in the plane at the finish.

One of the battles teachers face these days is the tendency for students to mimic specialty positions they see used by the pros. This includes things like the so-called abbreviated finish, a short follow-through where the hands only briefly get above head height. This finish is being employed by a number of Tour players these days. Tiger's mastery of this shot is well-documented. Phil Mickelson used it to perfection in his 2004 Masters victory and again in his second-place finish at the 2004 U.S. Open. During both those televised events, expert swing analysts commented on how the shortened finish had helped Mickelson's game. That was true, but it doesn't mean you should shorten your finish.

Phil Mickelson, Tiger Woods, and certainly many others have all worked on the abbreviated finish when they wanted to lower the trajectory of their shots and cut down on the amount of backspin. These are admirable and worthwhile goals for Tour players, but all these players worked hard to perfect a tall, balanced, and on-plane follow-through and finish, first. The last thing beginners need to be thinking about is a low shot, without spin. That's probably their normal ball flight anyway. They have a "short" finish (not to be confused with "abbreviated"), and it may feel okay, because they've seen it on TV. In reality, they do not finish high because they *can't* finish high. They've never trained themselves to finish there. For you to try to take the spin off your

9 iron with an abbreviated swing (a "knockdown"—more golfspeak) before you perfect the seventh fundamental position is like learning to fly an airplane by jumping into the cockpit of an advanced jet fighter. Your learning curve will be slow and your results ridiculous.

Here's a way to create a positive mental image of a tall, on-balance finish. This popular finish concept spawned the nickname *vogue* finish (a reference to being on the cover of the popular fashion magazine). When a player stays on balance, holding his finish until the ball hits the ground, you'll hear the TV commentators point out, "He's holding his finish, Johnny; he must like it." "He's voguing it!"

Learn to finish on plane first. Once you perfect this balanced follow-through, you can move on to more creative shot-shaping techniques. I like to remember it this way: Finish *on* balance, *on* plane, as though I were *on* TV.

Finish Healthy

In addition to hitting better golf shots, your biggest motivation for finishing tall and on balance is your health, particularly the strength and stamina of the lumbar region of your back. The torque of the golf swing puts enormous pressure on your lower back. That is why so many of the drills in this book emphasize strengthening and stretching the lumbar. Back injuries can kill your game forever. You should do whatever you can to avoid them.

A tall, balanced, and on-plane finish minimizes stress on the lumbar by elongating the torso. This distributes the pressure of the follow-through from your shoulders to your toes, instead of concentrating those pressures in your lower back.

Many of the previous workouts in this book will benefit your finish. Adding the physioball will improve your core strength and flexibility, simultaneously forcing you to concentrate on balance and coordination. Here are more specifics that will help you finish tall, balanced, and on plane.

One-Armed **Swing**

A

B

C

D

To get a feel for your arms folding as your shoulders turn through to the finish, hold the club in your left hand and grip your left forearm just above your wrist with your right hand. Take a few swings to feel the left arm releasing the club before folding at the elbow and then raising the club above your left shoulder (A, B).

After 20 swings holding the club in your left hand, put your right hand on the club and grip your right forearm just above the wrist with your left hand. A few swings from here will give you the feel for the right arm straightening and releasing the club at impact, extending the club down the target line, and continuing that extension around the body to the finish (C, D). This also keeps your right shoulder high through impact, extension, and finish—all critical components of a "tall" golf swing.

FINISH

Opposite-Arm-and-Leg **Raise**

A

B

For a challenging balance and stabilizing workout, hold a medicine ball and stand and bend at the waist until your upper body is at a 45-degree angle to the floor (A).

Now, straighten your left arm out in front of you while raising and straightening your right leg behind you (B). Both your raised arm and leg should be parallel to the floor. This keeps your core muscles tight and alert as you stand on one foot.

Alternate legs and arms, doing this 10 to 15 times on each side.

Swing **with a Blindfold**

A

B

To engage the sense of feel during the finish of your golf swing, compromise one of your other, more dominant senses. Try swinging with one of your eyes closed. If you have trouble with this, put on a blindfold and take some half or three-quarter swings. Once you feel comfortable with this

motion, extend your swing until you are taking full swings without the benefit of sight (A,B).

Ten to 20 swings with one of your eyes closed will do wonders for your balance and feel when you reengage your full sense of sight.

Waist-High to Finish
on Medicine Ball

A

B

To perfect the feelings of finishing tall and in balance, set up with your right foot on a medicine ball. Now swing the club to waist height on the backswing (A), and follow through to a full finish (B). The ball will force you to stand tall and balanced throughout the swing.

After 20 swings with your right foot on the medicine ball, put the ball under your left foot and make 20 swings (C, D). These swings will be harder because your body isn't accustomed to staying balanced. But performing this from both sides is important not only for balance in your golf swing but also for balance in your overall muscle development.

C   D

What to Expect

Sure, the ball is well on its way by the time momentum pulls the club to the top of
the finish. But consciously focusing on the finish by remaining tall, balanced, and on
plane throughout the follow-through will have had a positive effect on your entire
swing. If you work on the finish, the parts of your pre-impact swing will fall into
place, and the quality of your golf shots will improve dramatically.

Just vogue it.

STRETCHES

All
the exercises in this book
will improve strength and flexibility
and extend the range of motion needed in
a good golf swing. I've separated stretches into
this chapter because they apply to all seven positions, and because you can and should perform this
stretching regimen every day. In fact, the more
strengthening exercises you add to your daily and
weekly workouts, the more *absolutely essential*
quality stretching becomes. Regardless of your
work schedule, your practice and playing
schedule, or the hectic schedule of your
family life, you should carve out 15 to
25 minutes a day to stretch.
Not only will

your golf game improve, you will feel better about everything you do.

Few of us actually find a Zen inner peace through yogalike stretching. In fact, most of us just find inner soreness. What I will freely acknowledge, from personal experience and years of teaching, is that better flexibility leads to a more positive mental and emotional outlook. This may very well come from seeing positive athletic results, hence a more positive mental attitude. This makes complete sense to me. Certainly, the flip side is true (poor performance, poor mental outlook).

Stretching on a regular, if not daily basis is truly doable. I try to begin and end every day by stretching. If I work out during the day, I leave enough time at the end of my session to stretch the warm muscles I've just exercised. And if I'm playing golf in the afternoon, I carve out a few minutes for another series of stretches. This might be a good time to reread my second rule for getting in Golf Shape, on page 16, outlining how you should prioritize your stretching time during your pre-round warmups.

For some of you, this may seem like a hefty time commitment, but in truth, it may actually be just a fraction of the time that most Americans spend watching fast-food commercials or standing in line at Starbucks. Proper stretching really doesn't take much time. Despite proclamations to the contrary, medical research shows that holding a stretch for more than 30 seconds provides little or no additional benefit. Twenty minutes is all you need to complete a full complement of stretches that will leave you feeling great and swinging better.

Some of these stretches can be done with no assistance. Others require a rope, a bath towel, or a golf club. All of them should be done in the order they are shown, and performed without a break. If you work the program in this fashion, your muscles will be warmed, stretched, and ready in about the same time it will take you to read this chapter.

Hand, Wrist, and Forearm **Stretch**

Wrap a rope, belt, or a towel around the fingers of your left hand so that when you extend your arm palm up, the ends hang down evenly. (If you do not have a prop available, just use your opposite hand.) Now, grab the ends of the rope with your right hand and pull your fingers down until they point to the floor. Keep your arm straight and deepen the stretch by pulling your arm as far back as possible.

You will feel this in the palmaris longus (the long muscle that runs along the interior of your forearm) and the flexor carpi radialis (also an interior forearm muscle), as well as in the biceps.

Hold this stretch for 20 to 30 seconds with each arm.

Exterior Forearm **Stretch**

Keeping your left arm extended as you did in the hand, wrist, and forearm stretch, rotate your hand palm down, and wrap the rope or towel around the palm of your hand. Grab the ends with your right hand and pull until your fingers are pointing to the sky.

You will feel this in the muscles of the outer forearm. These include the extensor carpi radialis, longis, and brevis, and the supinator. Hold the stretch for 20 to 30 seconds with each arm for maximum effect.

Forearm Stretch with Golf Club

Hold a golf club in your left hand with the clubhead on the floor and your arm at your side.

Now, hinge at the wrist, lifting the club as far off the ground as you can. Once you have lifted the club as far as possible, place your right hand on the shaft and gently pull the club upward, extending your range of motion.

You will feel this stretch in the flexor carpi ulnaris (the muscle that runs along the bottom of your forearm) and in the tendons of your wrist. Hold the stretch for 20 to 30 seconds with each hand.

Triceps and Shoulder **Stretch**

Grab the clubhead in your left hand and place it behind your head so that the shaft of the club runs down your spine. Your left elbow should be level with your left ear. Now, reach behind your back with your right hand and grab the grip just above your hips. Pull down on the club with your right hand, stretching your left triceps and shoulder for 20 to 30 seconds. Switch hands and repeat.

Shoulder and Chest **Stretch**

A

B

C

Whether you use a stretching rope, towel, or golf club (driver) for this one will depend on your level of flexibility. Start with a rope or towel, grabbing each end and pulling it taut in front of your chest (A). Now, lift it over your head (B), behind your back and toward your hips (C) without bending your elbows. At first, you may not make it too far behind your head. In time, your flexibility and range of motion will improve.

At first, your hands will be pretty far apart. In time, your goal should be to move

your hands as close together as possible. This opens your chest and stretches your pectoralis, your front deltoids, and your rotator cuffs.

When you become flexible enough to perform this stretch with your hands 40 inches apart, drop the rope and use a golf club. Phil Mickelson is flexible enough to perform this stretch with a wedge, the shortest club in his bag.

I recommend that you do 10 slow reps.

Rotator Cuff **Stretch**

A

B

With your palms down and your arms straight, hold a golf club in front of you with one hand near the clubhead and the other near the grip (A).

Now, rotate the club clockwise until your arms have crossed (B). You will feel this stretch in your left rotator cuff. Hold it for 20 to 30 seconds before rotating the club counterclockwise to stretch the right rotator cuff.

Deltoid **Stretch**

A

B

Standing in a doorway or to the left of another vertical support, reach your left arm across your chest and grab the support with your left hand (A). Now, keep your arm straight and lean to your left. It may help to place your feet close to the support you are grasping. You will feel this stretch in the center and rear deltoid. It is sometimes hard to find this stretch, so focus on the muscles of your shoulder and lean slowly to your left until you feel it in the center and rear of your left shoulder. Hold that stretch for 20 to 30 seconds and repeat with the right arm (B).

Rotational Pillar **Stretch**

In the same doorway, turn your back to the door frame and rotate your shoulders clockwise until you can grab the molding with both hands. Now rotate your hips counterclockwise. You will feel this stretch throughout the left side of your torso, and also in your left shoulder, arm, and hip.

Hold this position for 20 to 30 seconds, and then change sides, rotating your shoulders counterclockwise and your hips clockwise to stretch your right side.

Oblique **Stretch**

A

B

C

Hold a golf club straight over your head with your arms extended. One hand should be near the grip and the other near the clubhead (A).

Now, lean to your right, effectively hinging at the right hip, keeping your head centered between your arms and your feet on the floor (B). You are very effectively stretching your left oblique. When you have leaned as far as possible, pull the club downward with your right hand to deepen the stretch.

You should feel this in your left lateral oblique, latissimus dorsi, middle trapezius, and teres major, all the muscles that affect your motion on the left side of your torso.

Once you've held the stretch for 20 to 30 seconds, slowly return to the start position and lean to the left, pulling with your left hand to deepen the stretch on your right side (C).

Abdominal **Stretch**

A

B

Lie facedown on the floor with your hands flat as though you were about to do a pushup (A).

Now, keeping your hips, legs, and toes on the floor, lift your chest and shoulders. You will feel this throughout your abdominal re-gion and across your lower lumbar region. Tilt your head back and look at the ceiling to intensify the stretch. Hold for 20 to 30 seconds. For a more advanced stretch, lift your chest and shoulders until your arms are straight (B).

Lower-Back **Stretch**

Roll over onto your back and pull your knees into your chest. Clasp your hands behind your knees (or wrap your arms in front of your knees) and pull while lifting your head and shoulders. Pull your knees as close as you can to your ears, and hold the stretch for 20 to 30 seconds.

Upper (Rounded) Back **Stretch**

Stand a couple of feet away from the footboard of your bed or any vertical object that will support your body weight. Put your hands close together and hold the footboard as you bend your legs and squat into your heels, as shown. Round your back and push your glutes back and toward the floor.

Hold for 20 to 30 seconds.

This stretches the latissimus dorsi; upper, middle, and lower trapezius; infraspinatus; longissimus; and iliocostalis (all the muscles of the upper back that control your spine angle throughout the swing).

Neck Stretch **with Resistance**

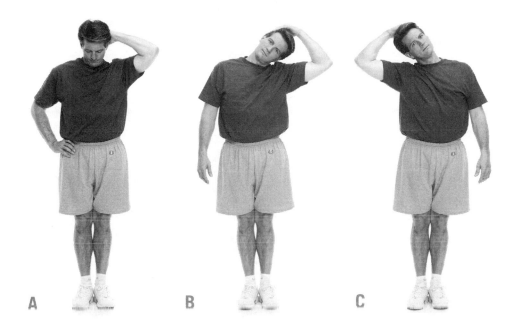

A   **B**   **C**

From a standing position, lower your head and look at floor. Put your left hand on the back of your head and push gently to stretch the muscles around your neck (A).

After 20 seconds, move your hand to the right side of your head to stretch the muscles on the right side of your neck (B).

Then use your right hand to stretch the left side (C).

Calf **Stretch**

From a seated position with your legs extended, place your stretching aid across the ball of your foot and pull both ends, forcing your toes back toward your shin. You will feel this in your calf and Achilles tendon.

Hold it for 20 to 30 seconds, then move immediately on to the hamstring stretch.

Hamstring **Stretch**

Don't remove the rope from your foot. Slide it down into your arch and lie on your back, on the floor. Now, pull on the rope, raising your leg without bending at the knee. Pull your toes as close as you can to your forehead without flexing your knee.

Your hamstrings might not let you lift your leg higher than perpendicular to the ground. That's okay. Pull on the rope to deepen the stretch as far as possible, and hold it for 20 to 30 seconds, then move immediately on to the glute stretch. If you work this stretch every day, you will see a measurable increase in your hamstring flexibility in a matter of weeks.

Glute **Stretch**

Without lowering your leg or removing the stretching aid, flex your knee slightly. This will allow you to pull your foot closer to your forehead. It also shifts the stretch from your hamstring to your glutes and lower back.

Hold this stretch for 20 to 30 seconds and move immediately to the deep hip stretch.

Deep Hip **Stretch**

Without lowering your leg from the glute stretch, take both ends of the rope or towel in your opposite hand and extend your arm to your side. Keeping your shoulders on the floor, cross your raised leg over the other.

You will feel this in the iliacus, psoas major, quadratus lumborum, tensor fasciae latae, and pectineus, muscles that control hip rotation and affect your lower back.

Hold this stretch for 20 to 30 seconds, then move immediately on to the quad stretch.

Quad **Stretch**

Immediately after releasing the deep hip stretch, roll onto your side, slide the rope onto the top of your upper foot, bend at the knee, and hold the ends of the strap in your upper hand. Now put your hand behind your head, and pull your heel toward your lower back. This stretches the quadriceps.

Hold this stretch for 20 to 30 seconds.

The rope- or towel-assisted leg stretches—calf, hamstring, glute, deep hip, and quad—should have taken 2½ minutes. Move the stretching aid to the other foot and repeat the previous five stretches on that side. The entire process takes 5 minutes and stretches most of the major muscle groups below the waist. Then do the following groin stretch.

Groin **Stretch**

Sit on the floor, put the soles of your feet together, and draw your feet as close to your hips as possible. Now, put your forearms on the insides of your thighs and press your knees toward the floor as you lean your torso forward.

You will feel this in the gracilis and sartorius muscles, commonly called the groin. Hold this stretch for 20 to 30 seconds.

The previous movements, performed in order, progressively stretch every muscle used in the golf swing. They are not a substitute for the exercises outlined in the rest of the book, but should be a complement to your new golf-specific regimen.

Remember, stretch every day. No exceptions and no excuses. And never, *never* play or practice without doing your favorite abbreviated stretching routine first. The following program takes less than 15 minutes in its entirety.

Abbreviated Pre-Round Stretching

It is absolutely essential to include a stretching routine in every pre-round (or practice) warmup. This should never take more than 10 to 15 minutes. I place nearly equal priority on lengthening and loosening muscles, tendons, and ligaments as on hitting practice balls before the round. Given only enough time to do one or the other, I'll stretch (and roll a few putts, of course).

Here's a simple 15-minute (maximum) routine to send you off to the first tee or practice facility ready to hit quality shots. (These stretches will *not* require you to lie on the ground).

The first 5 to 10 minutes: I like to flex the muscles of my fingers and hands, clenching and opening my fists. I roll my wrist from palm up to palm down, while rolling my fist around its maximum range of motion. To intensify this motion, I hold two or three clubs in the centers of the shafts and roll my wrist around slowly. This should just take a minute.

Stretching the shoulders is next, ranking high in importance. First, extend your arms straight out to the sides (parallel to the ground), palms up. Make 10 to 15 small circles in the air with your hands, slowly increasing the size of the circles (A).

A

The initial direction of rotation is not important, as long as you reverse the direction to complete the stretch. Next, with your arms still outstretched to the sides (and still palms up), rotate your shoulders and upper torso 90 degrees, putting one arm directly in front and one in back. This will stretch your lower torso to the position necessary to complete a full shoulder turn. There is no hold time for this stretch. It is only important to gradually try to increase the range of motion.

Now, as a variation of this rotational stretch, place your driver across the top of your shoulders and grasp both ends (B). Rotate your shoulders in each direction 90 degrees or more, pressing against your range of motion limits for just a few seconds. Accomplish all of these torso stretches slowly and deliberately.

B   C

Now, bending at the hip sockets (keeping your knees slightly flexed), repeat the upper-body rotation to 90 degrees in both directions (C). You have now effectively stretched on the same shoulder plane as your golf swing. By now, you will feel your range of motion increasing.

Let's finish the upper body with one of Jack Nicklaus's favorites. With your right hand, reach over your left arm and grab your elbow. While holding your shoulders and arms level, pull your left arm straight across in front of your chest (D). Hold this for 10 to 20 seconds. Repeat this for your right arm and shoulder.

D

Next, hold your driver head with your left hand, and position it behind your head with the shaft running down your spine. Reach behind your back with your right hand, grabbing the grip. Pull the club straight down toward the ground while keeping your left elbow pointed straight in front of you (E). Hold for 10 seconds. This is an effective way to stretch the top of your shoulder and triceps. Switch hands and repeat.

E

Next, let's open up the chest and stretch the sides. Keeping the driver handy, grab it by the clubhead in one hand and the end of the grip in the other, using an overhand grip. Starting with the shaft in front of your thighs, raise it straight up and over your head, keeping your elbows straight throughout this entire movement (F). Stretch your arms behind your head, as far back as you can (no cheating—keep those elbows straight). At first, you may not be able to go very far back, but you are effectively stretching your chest and the fronts of your shoulders. Slowly bring the club back down to your thighs for one rep. Perform 10 reps, each time trying to extend your range of motion.

F

Finally, while still holding the driver over your head, bend over sideways, hinging at the hip (G). It is important to keep your arms and torso in one piece and your elbows straight. This is a great way to stretch the sides. Be sure to do this in both directions, 5 to 10 reps on each side.

Your upper body is now ready to go.

G

The last 5 minutes: Warming up for any athletic endeavor requires stretching your legs, the very foundation of your golf swing. Let's stretch these long, strong muscles.

First, I like the classic runner's calf stretch. Using any stationary object (a wall, a tree, or Charles Barkley), place both hands against the object with one leg well behind the other and straightened, keeping that foot absolutely flat on the ground (H). Emphasizing a flat heel, allow your body to slowly lean closer to the wall. You will feel the calf muscles stretch. Hold this stretch for 20 to 30 seconds, then repeat with the other leg.

H

Now, let's talk hamstrings. Remain standing, and take the ends of your golf towel in each hand. Raise your toes off the ground enough to slip the towel underneath. Bending over at the hips, while maintaining a straight back and little or no knee flex, pull on the towel (I). Attempt to touch your chest to your thighs (only very flexible people can actually do this). The more you pull (closing the gap between your chest and thighs) the more your hamstrings will stretch. Hold this position at the limit of your range of motion for 10 to 20 seconds.

I

Now, let's finish with stretching the quads (front thighs). While standing, lift one foot behind you (heel toward glutes), bend at the hips, and grab your ankle with your opposite hand. Straighten your body while pulling your ankle upward, toward your backside (J). You will now resemble a flamingo (although you should not be pink). Consider using a club or nearby stationary object to maintain your balance. As you pull upward, you should feel your quadriceps stretch. Maintain this tension for 10 to 20 seconds. Repeat with the opposite leg.

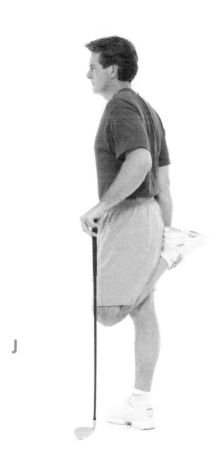

J

Before you head out to practice, turn the page and let's wrap up with some driving range drills that help piece together the seven fundamental golf positions into one fluid swing.

RANGE DRILLS

Coupled
with instruction from a
qualified PGA or LPGA teaching
professional, the workouts outlined in these
pages will condition your body to find the seven
fundamental positions of a great swing. But you
still have to practice. The drills in this book are no
substitute for a thoughtful, efficient, goal-oriented
practice routine on the range. Toned golf muscles
make practicing easier, but you still have to spend
time on the range, swinging, sweating, and
learning. You can feel great about your progress
after a good workout in the gym or your
living room. Sitting at your desk, it's
easy to think you've "got it,"
as you're

getting more and more fit. But the only feeling that matters is the one you get when your clubface makes solid contact and the ball flies long, straight, and right at your target. How do you get there? The practice tee.

Here are some driving range drills that will help you find that feeling more often.

The first two drills, for uphill and downhill lies, presuppose that you have access to a facility that has any significant slope from which to practice. Occasionally, you can find the edge of a practice tee where an elevated hitting area has been shaped, and create your own sloped lies. A little imagination and a friendly range manager helps a lot here.

Hit a Bucket of Balls
from an Uphill Lie

Chris Cordon/PGA Tour

Nothing exposes flaws in your setup, take-away, and weight shift through impact like an unusual lie. I suggest hitting at least one bag or bucket (40 to 50 balls) from an up-hill lie (using a variety of clubs) with your left foot above your right. This unusual lie forces you to think about things like spine angle, shoulder tilt (matching the slope), and weight distribution at address. The nat-ural physics of this setup promotes a some-what inside-to-outside swing path. This is a wonderful scenario for those of us whose tendency is the outside-to-in (casting) swing path. Gravity forces you to load most of your weight on your right side at the top of the backswing. Uphill lies also force you

to drive your weight forward through im-pact. If you don't make a concerted effort to rotate your hips and positively shift your weight to the left side, you will hang back and hit the shot fat, or at least way, way left of the target.

If you shift your weight properly in both directions and keep your spine angle con-stant throughout the swing, you should an-ticipate a nice high draw from the upslope. It's a shot worth practicing, even if you rarely have uphill lies on your course. Practicing from an upslope pays dividends across the board, not just for the occasional uphill shot you may encounter.

Hit a Bucket of Balls
from a Downhill Lie

Chris Condon/PGA Tour

While hitting from an uphill lie forces you to load your weight onto your right leg at the top, hitting from a downhill lie is an equally effective technique to emphasize hitting down and through the ball. What is critical here is the extension through the hitting area. Weight transfer to the left side is virtually automatic, once again, due to gravity. There is usually not a significant right or left issue here, just a guaranteed lower ball flight. Once again, it is imperative to match your shoulder tilt to the slope of the hill. Crucial to either of the drills is balance, balance, balance.

I emphasize this drill to just about all my students, from high-handicappers to Tour professionals. Everyone can benefit from hitting 20 to 30 balls from a downhill lie during each practice session.

Step into the Shot
to Feel Rotation and Weight Shift

Chris Condon/PGA Tour

No matter how many off-course drills I prescribe, most amateurs still have trouble beginning the downswing with their hips. One of the best driving range drills I've found for getting the feel of this action is to set up with your feet *together* and step into the shot as you start your downswing.

This drill emphasizes several critical feelings during the swing: By taking your backswing with your feet together, you are more likely to make a full shoulder turn around a steady right leg. Stepping into the shot forces you to initiate the downswing below your waist. Momentum forces you to shift your weight. And your footwork ensures that you will focus on your balance throughout the swing. Don't worry about perfect ball contact initially, during this drill. The goal is weight transfer and balance.

This is also a drill I prescribe for players of all ages and skill levels. It benefits Tour players and beginners alike. Hitting about 10 solid shots will make my point.

Hit Balls **from Your Knees**

Chris Condon/PGA Tour

Jim Flick and I aren't the only ones who practice hitting balls from our knees. Former Tour pro and current CBS analyst Bobby Clampett can hit 250-yard drives while on his knees, and Vijay Singh can shape shots on command from a kneeling position. While you might never reach this level of proficiency, you should spend some time hitting balls from your knees.

This drill forces you to swing with the large core muscles of your torso and shoulders. If you attempt to manipulate the club with your hands and arms, you will stick the clubhead in the ground well behind the ball. Again, about 10 balls, struck squarely, should be enough here.

Lift Your Right Foot and Hold Your Finish until the Ball Hits the Ground

Chris Condon/PGA Tour

To ensure a tall, balanced finish with your weight shifted to your left side, lift your right foot off the ground on your follow-through, and hold your finish until the ball hits the ground.

Most amateurs (and a few pros) have to catch their balance the first few times they try this drill. But after hitting 20 to 30 practice balls with this finish, you will feel what I mean by a tall and balanced finish.

What to Expect

Your teaching professional will have more drills that deal with things specific to your golf swing. But if you incorporate these drills into your regular practice sessions, you will positively reinforce the normal setups and shots you'll be working on most of the time.

11-DAY GOLF SHAPE PROGRAM

Any
serious goal in life requires
a dedicated plan, one with realistic
milestones and attainable results. Here's
an 11-day fitness plan that incorporates the exercises, stretches, and driving range drills you've
learned on the previous pages. It is specially designed
to strengthen and retrain your body for each of the
seven key swing positions we have discussed.
All the exercises offered here will improve your ability
to achieve the seven fundamental positions. As you
begin to do the more advanced versions of the exercises, you will strengthen critical muscle
groups that stabilize the key positions
and more effectively accelerate
the golf club.

How to Use This Program

The order in which I recommend doing each day's exercises and stretches is not a hard-and-fast regimen. You can tailor the sequence to your preferences. This latitude applies to the entire 11-day workout program.

Obviously, a fitness program cannot be complete without dedicated stretching. *Stretching can help your golf game overnight.* Period. I feel that strongly about it.

As you may have noticed, I recommend stretches in two different capacities within this book. Some stretches are included only in the Stretches chapter because they apply to all seven of the fundamental positions. Others are included in the individual position chapters, such as the hip crossover stretch in the Setup chapter. That's because the latter type are targeted specifically to the position discussed in each chapter. Essentially, these are less strenuous, more basic versions of related strengthening exercises. So, for example, in the Setup chapter, the hip crossover stretch becomes the hip crossover and the hip crossover with physioball—both strengthening exercises, yet built on the basic stretch.

I cannot overemphasize how important it is to stretch before any strenuous workout. I recommend performing some, if not all, of the stretches outlined each day prior to each set of exercises.

Start your stretching regimen slowly, gently, and deliberately, as cold muscles resist stretching.

It is always appropriate (especially when doing advanced exercises) to also include stretching between exercises. While the specific stretches mentioned for a given day are appropriate, any method of warming a muscle group is better than no stretching at all.

After you exercise, complete your daily workouts with cooldown stretching to loosen and relax the muscle groups you have just taxed. An abbreviated version of the stretches you accomplished prior to the workout should be sufficient here.

Volumes have been written about the positive benefits of aerobic conditioning, and I couldn't agree more. That's why this program gives you the opportunity to insert your favorite cardiovascular workouts into the mix. Where and how you add them is, for the most part, up to you, though, as you'll see, I recommend Day 4 as a good time. Doing *any* aerobic exercise, *anywhere* in the program, will only enhance this fitness regimen and is vastly better than doing none at all. If your knees, back, and ankles are in reasonable shape, consider jogging or fast walking. Should a lower-impact workout be more to your taste, think bicycling, a rowing machine, or my favorite, swimming laps. Any of these time-honored activities, when executed with sufficient vigor to sustain an elevated heart rate for 30 or more minutes, will provide the aerobic conditioning to complement your exercise and stretching program.

Finally, it's important to take the recommended days off to rest. There are several reasons for this. Chief among them is to avoid overtraining. Exercised muscles need rest and recovery to actually increase their capacity to do work. Additionally, without days off, your workouts may become the goal, rather than a way to achieve the goal (that is, a more powerful, technically correct swing). Remember, in a fairly short period of time, bad habits can be replaced with good ones.

Any athletic endeavor is improved with physical conditioning. As today's Tour pros clearly demonstrate, golf is certainly no exception. This program is not a stand-alone way to lower your scores. It is a complement to your practice routines. If you use it that way, stick to it, and commit to being a better, stronger player, you will improve your ball striking, get more enjoyment from the game, and—lo and behold—lower your scores.

Day 1
Position One: Setup

Stretches

Hip Crossover
Stretch (page 35):
10 to 15 reps on
each side

A

B

C

Abdominal Stretch
(page 168): hold
for 20 to 30 sec-
onds

A

B

Oblique Stretch
(page 167): hold
for 20 to 30
seconds on each
side

A

B

C

Back Extension
Stretch (page 43):
10 to 15 reps

A

B

Exercises
The Kitchen Chair
(page 31): 10 to
12 reps

A   B

Soccer-Ball
Squeeze (page
32): hold for 30
seconds

A

Hip Crossover
(page 36): 10 to
15 reps on each
side

A   B   C

Oblique Crunch,
(page 38): 10 to
15 reps

A   B

Reverse Crunch,
(page 41): 10 to
15 reps

A   B

Back Extension
with Physioball
(page 44): 3 sets
of 10 to 15 reps

A   B

Day 2
Position Two: Initial Takeaway

Stretches
Overhead Shoulder
Stretch (page 60):
10 reps

A

B

C

Bent-Waist Fly
Stretch (page 63):
10 to 15 reps

A

Oblique Stretch
(page 167): hold
for 20 to 30 sec-
onds on each side

A

B

C

Back Extension
Stretch (page 43):
10 to 15 reps

A

B

Exercises
Chair-to-Counter
Reach (page 54):
10 to 12 reps

A

B

Seated Hands-to-Floor Reach (page 55): 10 to 12 reps on each side

A

B

C

D

Seated Rotational Pull (In Gym), page 57: 10 reps on each side

A

B

Lat Pull (In Gym), page 59: 2 sets of 8 to 10 reps

A

B

Overhead Shoulder Stretch with Weight (page 62): 10 to 15 reps

A

B

C

Bent-Waist Fly with Resistance (page 64): 3 sets of 10 to 15 reps

A

B

Day 3
Position Three: Top of the Backswing

Stretches
Chair-Turn Stretch
(page 75): hold for
30 seconds on
each side

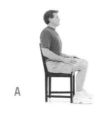

A

B

C

Left-Hand
Handshake Stretch
(page 76): hold for
30 seconds

A

Exercises
Medicine Ball
Rotation (page
77): 10 reps

A

B

C

Step and Reach
(page 78): 5 to 10
reps

A

B

Kneeling
Rotational Pull (In
Gym), page 80: 10
to 12 reps on each
side

A

B

Swing with Left
Foot on Medicine
Ball (page 81): 5
to 8 reps

A

Touch and Toss
(page 82): 10 reps
on each side

A   B   C

Day 4
Cardio and Stretching

This represents a day off from strengthening, allowing your muscles to recover. It's a good day to do your cardiovascular workout and the stretching program outlined in the Stretches chapter (excluding the pre-round routine).

Day 5
Position Four: Initial Downswing

Stretches
Door Frame Pull
Stretch (page 92):
hold for two 20-
second reps on
each side

Neck Stretch with
Resistance (page
171): hold for 20
seconds in each
position

Rotator Cuff
Stretch (page
164): hold for 20
to 30 seconds on
each side

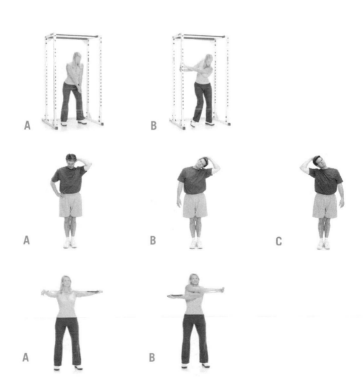

Hamstring Stretch (page 173): hold for 20 to 30 seconds on each side

A

Quad Stretch (page 175): hold for 20 to 30 seconds on each side

A

Exercises
Standing Rotational Pull (page 93): 10 to 12 reps on each side

A   B

Pillar Stabilizer Pushup (page 94): 3 sets of 10 to 12 reps

A   B

Pillar Rotation (page 95): 5 reps on each side

A   B   C

Side Stabilizer Hip Lift (page 96): three 20-second reps on each side

A   B

Physio Squat (page 97): 10 reps

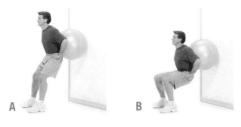

Front Lunge (page 99): 10 reps on each side

Back Rotational Lunge with Golf Club (page 102): 10 reps on each side

The following explosive exercises are all advanced moves and are therefore optional.

Rotating Jump (Advanced), page 103: as many as possible in 60 seconds

Explosive Step (Advanced), page 105: on each side, as many reps as possible in 30 seconds

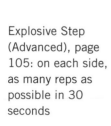

Explosive Step with Medicine Ball (Advanced), page 106: on each side, as many reps as possible in 30 seconds

Lateral Leap with Medicine Ball (Advanced), page 104: as many reps as possible in 60 seconds

Day 6
Review

You have just completed a fairly strenuous workout on Day 5. Today should be considered a light day, a nice balance. Reflect on the exercises and stretches you performed over the last several days—for Setup, Takeaway, Top of the Backswing, and Initial Downswing—and work on those that you found the most difficult. Remember, form and precision of each exercise is always more important than the amount of weight you lifted or the number of repetitions you completed. As always, stretch, stretch, stretch. You choose which ones. Obviously, focus on those you hate.

Day 7
Rest

Take a break. Go roll some putts! (I'm sorry, I meant go make some putts.)

Day 8
Position Five: Impact

Stretches

Abdominal Stretch
(page 168): hold
for 20 to 30
seconds

A

B

Lower-Back Stretch
(page 169): hold
for 20 to 30
seconds

A

Upper (Rounded)
Back Stretch (page
170): hold for 20
to 30 seconds

A

Calf Stretch (page
172): hold for 20
to 30 seconds on
each side

A

Glute Stretch (page
174) hold for 20 to
30 seconds on
each side

A

Deep Hip Stretch
(page 174): hold
for 20 to 30
seconds on each
side

A

Exercises

Wrist Club Lift (page 117): 15 to 20 reps on each side

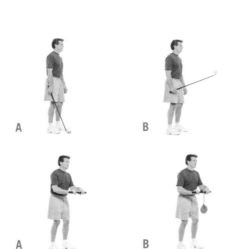

A B

Wrist Roll (page 118): 8 to 10 reps

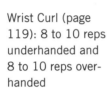

A B

Wrist Curl (page 119): 8 to 10 reps underhanded and 8 to 10 reps overhanded

A B

Wrist Rotation (page 120): 8 to 10 reps

A B

Situp Toss (page 121): 10 reps

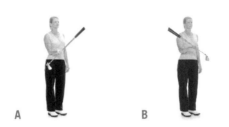

A B C

Weighted Driver (page 122): 3 sets of 15 to 20 reps

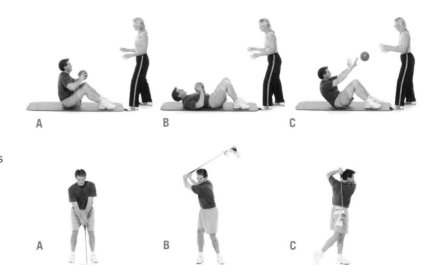

A B C

Crossover Cable Pull (In Gym), page 124: 10 reps on each side

A   B   C

Leg Curl (page 126): 3 sets of 10 reps

A   B

Day 9
Positions Six and Seven: Extension and Finish

There are two strength training workouts I recommend to help your post-impact extension and finish. Additionally, by focusing on stretching and strengthening those muscle groups which promoted better rotation and extension to the right, and emphasizing them in the opposite (left) side, you will complete this "hip-high to hip-high" package. Here are my favorite exercises to help promote a longer extension through the hitting area.

Swing a Broom to a Waist-High Finish (page 134): 30 reps

A   B

Extend the Shaft Up the Left Side (page 135): 20 reps

A   B   C   D

The following exercises are beneficial to overall golf fitness, extension, and balance. This is a good day to include them. They are:

Bicycle (page 136): 10 reps on each side

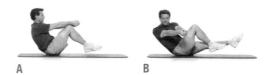

A   B

Toe Raise (page 138): 15 reps

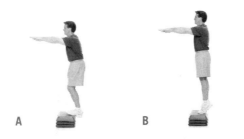

A   B

Abductor Lift (page 139): 10 to 15 reps on each side

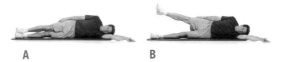

A   B

Adductor Lift (page 140): 10 to 15 reps on each side

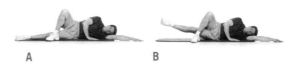

A   B

One-Armed Swing
(page 151): 20
reps on each side

A   B

C   D

Opposite-Arm-and-
Leg Raise (page
152): 10 to 15
reps on each side

A   B

Swing with a
Blindfold (page
153): 10 to 20
reps

A   B

Waist-High to
Finish on Medicine
Ball (page 154):
20 reps on each
side

A   B

C   D

Swing with Left
Foot on Medicine
Ball (page 81): 5
to 8 reps

A

Day 10
Rest, but Stretch

This is a great day to review the Abbreviated Pre-Round Stretching routine (used at the golf course, prior to practicing or playing) starting on page 177. By practicing this routine at home, you will proceed through it quickly and smoothly at the course. You will find that it emphasizes many of the more involved stretches we've discussed earlier but in an abbreviated, self-contained format. The only equipment you'll need is a golf club and a golf towel. From beginning to end, you'll have a fine 10- to 15-minute workout. Then, go roll some quality putts.

Day 11
Tie It Together

On the last day of your 11-day program, take it to the range. Once there, go through your pre-round stretching routine, then launch into the range drills described starting on page 187. Here are some examples of how the workouts and stretches you completed over the past 10 days will translate to improvements in your range drills.

1. Your hip and glute stretches will have helped stabilize your lower body, keeping you balanced on your uphill- and downhill-lie drills.

2. The hamstring and quad stretches will have freed up that leg drive for your rotation and weight-shift drill.

3. Upper-body, shoulder-rotation, and range-of-motion stretches will make themselves evident in the hitting-from-your-knees drill.

4. The exercises swing with one eye closed and swing with left foot on medicine ball (in which your foot is elevated to focus on weight transfer), along with the range drill lift your right foot and hold your finish until the ball hits the ground will certainly improve your appreciation for balance, a critical element in all facets of the swing.

I think you are getting my point. There are a nearly endless number of applications of the aforementioned drills and stretches that apply to an improved golf swing. Be creative and find some more for yourself.

The Twelfth Day and Beyond

So what do you do after Day 11? The wonderful thing about this program is that you never outgrow it. After you finish your first 11 days, take a few days "off" and play golf, rest a bit, get in some cardio and stretching. Then, repeat the program from the beginning. As you improve, the basic moves eventually will become a bit too easy, will fail to fatigue targeted muscles, or will no longer challenge your range of motion. When this happens, increase the number of repetitions until you are doing the maximum number in a given range. When those reps, too, become easy, do additional sets as advised in the original description of each exercise. For exercises using weights such as dumbbells, medicine balls, or pulley machines, you should increase the amount of weight as your strength grows.

You'll recall that I provided advanced versions of some exercises. You will know the time has come to move on to the advanced versions when you can complete the maximum recommended number of sets and reps of the less strenuous, more basic exercises. The basic moves can then become your warmups. So the exercises would change as follows:

Position One: Setup

• Hip crossover becomes a warmup for the advanced hip crossover with physioball (page 37)

• Oblique crunch becomes a warmup for the advanced oblique crunch with physioball (page 39)

• Reverse crunch becomes a warmup for the advanced reverse crunch with physioball (page 42)

Position Two: Initial Takeaway

• Seated hands-to-floor reach becomes a warmup for the advanced seated weight-to-floor-reach (page 56)

• Bent-waist fly with resistance becomes a warmup for the advanced bent-waist fly with weights (page 65)

Position Three: Top of the Backswing

• Step and reach becomes a warmup for the advanced step and reach with medicine ball (page 79)

Position Four: Initial Downswing

• Pillar stabilizer pushup becomes a warmup for the advanced pillar rotation (page 95)

• Physio squat becomes a warmup for the advanced physio squat with medicine ball (page 98)

• Front lunge becomes a warmup for the advanced front lunge with golf club (page 100); when the latter gets too easy, it becomes the warmup and is followed by front lunge with medicine ball (page 101)

• If you haven't done them all already, begin adding the advanced, explosive exercises: rotating jump (page 103), lateral leap with medicine ball (page 104), explosive step (page 105), and explosive step with medicine ball (page 106)

Position Six: Extension

• Bicycle becomes a warmup for the advanced bicycle with medicine ball (page 137)

As your fitness continues to improve, you can continue to add reps and sets as well as weight to the exercises, add range of motion to the stretches, and add intensity to the explosive moves. So this same program can evolve into a lifetime golf-specific routine.

If you stick to this program, hit balls a couple of times a week, and take 10 to 15 lessons a year (especially if you take them from me, of course), you will close the gap between being a *potentially* good player and being a *really* good player. The confidence to take your new swing mechanics to the first tee will manifest itself as quickly as you are willing to build them into muscle memory. The pleasure and enjoyment this brings to the game is immeasurable.

CONCLUSION
WHAT TO EXPECT

Gary
Player, the godfather of
modern golf fitness and a personal
hero of mine, never misses an opportunity
to preach his message about staying fit for a
lifetime. At a Champions Tour event in Atlanta,
Gary turned a routine post-round practice session
into a clinic for the gallery behind the range.
"Look up and down this range," he shouted to the
crowd. "You'll not see anyone over 60 out here who
is really fat. That's because fat bodies wear out. The
Creator gave you a wonderful piece of ma-
chinery, and man created this wonderful
game we call golf. To play the game
forever, you have to keep your
body in shape.

I've done it. You can do it, too."

The crowd laughed and applauded as Gary hit one age-defying drive after another. His message was lost on no one.

Gary Player revolutionized the perception of professional golfers as athletes. At the peak of his career, his fitness regimen rivaled that of any athlete in the world. Because of his commitment to keeping his body in Golf Shape, Gary is the only man in history to win professional events in 6 different decades.

I can't tell you how good a golfer you will become. What I can tell you is that you will get out of the game what you put into it. If you will dedicate yourself to the program I've set forth in these pages, practice your game on a regular basis, seek professional advice frequently, and walk to the practice range or first tee with a positive attitude, your scoring *will* improve, and you'll come to better appreciate what Gary meant about "this wonderful game we call golf." Remember, lower scores are just the report card for all of your hard work. Being happier with your game and your life is the real goal here.

Okay, now get to work. There's a lifetime of good rounds out there waiting for you.

INDEX

Boldface page references indicate photographs.